YANGTZE

YANGTZE

PHILIP WILKINSON

BBC
BOOKS

This book is dedicated to the memory of Miriam Hyman

First published in 2005
Copyright © Philip Wilkinson 2005
The moral right of the author has been asserted

Published by BBC Books, BBC Worldwide Ltd,
Woodlands, 80 Wood Lane, London W12 0TT

ISBN 0 563 48779 8

Commissioning editors: Shirley Patton and Stuart Cooper

Edited and designed by Pippa Rubinstein and Judith Robertson (R & R Publishing)
Art director: Linda Blakemore
Picture researcher: Miriam Hyman
Production controllers: Alix McCulloch and David Brimble

Set in Helvetica Neue and Trajan
Colour origination and printing by
Butler & Tanner Ltd, Frome, England

TIMELINE

The most ancient evidence of early hominids in China has recently been discovered a few miles south of the Yangtze at Longgupo. Here fossil teeth some 1.9 million years old have been found. But for the origins of Chinese civilization, one has to look further north, to the banks of the Yellow River, where the Bronze Age Shang dynasty was based, and where the written history of China begins.

The kings of early dynasties such as the Shang controlled only parts of China. The first rulers to unite the whole country were the emperors of the Qin dynasty. Since their time, many subsequent ruling dynasties have tried, with varying results, to hold the vast land together and to protect it from outside invaders. The most successful dynasties, such as the Tang, Song and Ming, achieved this, as well as presiding over great achievements in the arts and sciences. But between these 'golden ages' were times of disunity, when rival families fought for control of China. The following list of China's ruling powers outlines these changes and notes the main achievements of each dynasty.

PRE-IMPERIAL PERIOD

Shang dynasty *c.* 1500–1045 BC

The country's first important dynasty presides over a Bronze Age civilization in which kings from northern China rule from walled cities and the distinctive Chinese style of writing is developed.

Zhou dynasty *c.* 1045–256 BC
    Western Zhou *c.* 1045–771 BC
    Eastern Zhou *c.* 770–256 BC
        Spring and Autumn period 722–481 BC
        Warring States period 480–222 BC

The Zhou kings develop a feudal system, with peasants working on large estates under the control of lords. Towards the end of this period, some of the lords fight in an attempt to gain supremacy. Many are killed and China is divided.

IMPERIAL PERIOD

Qin dynasty 221–207 BC

The first emperor, Qin Shihuangdi, unites China, builds the Great Wall, and standardizes currency, weights and measures, and the Chinese script. Hatred of the Qins' harsh laws and a crippling programme of public works mean that their rule is short-lived.

Han dynasty 206 BC–AD 220
    Western Han 206 BC–AD 23
    Eastern Han 25–200

The Han emperors install an effective civil service, which helps them keep power and remains at the heart of Chinese government for centuries. Increasingly, Confucianism becomes the central imperial philosophy.

The Three Kingdoms
    Wei 220–264
    Wu 222–280
    Shu 221-263

With the fall of the Han, China splits into separate kingdoms – the Wei in the north, the Wu in the south and the Shu in the west. The Yangtze, close to the northern border of the Wu territory, becomes the scene of battles between the rival states.

The Period of Disunity
    Western Jin dynasty 265–318
    Eastern Jin dynasty 317–419
    Liu Song dynasty 420–479
    Qi dynasty 479–501
    Liang dynasty 502–556
    Chen dynasty 557–618
	A succession of mainly military rulers tries to unite China, but most have only local power. Chinese political culture is transformed by the influence of northern 'barbarians', while religious life is changed with the increasing popularity of Buddhism.

Sui dynasty 581–618	The founder of the Sui dynasty, Wendi, reunites China, banning private armies and strengthening the administration. The Sui emperors create the Grand Canal, linking the Yangtze and Yellow rivers and improving communications between north and south.
Tang dynasty 618–907	Building on the success of the Sui, the Tang emperors turn China into a major power. This is also a time of cultural brilliance, in which the arts, from poetry to porcelain, flourish, and trade along the major rivers expands.

The Five Dynasties 907–960
    Later Laing 907–923
    Later Tang 923–935
    Later Jin 936–947
    Later Han 947–951
    Later Zhou 951–960
	With the fall of the Tang, China splits up once more. Foreign rulers dominate the north, but the southern area, around the Yangtze, is more prosperous. The Five Dynasties are dogged by usurpation and murder, and are all short-lived.

Song dynasty 960–1279
    Northern Song 960–1126
    Southern Song 1127–1279
	Under the Song, China is once more united. Power starts to shift from the aristocracy to the middle classes, and Chinese culture and scholarship are revived. Industry flourishes, with material such as iron produced on a large scale.

Yuan dynasty 1279–1368	China is conquered by the Mongols, who establish the Yuan dynasty. Trade, especially along the Silk Road, is developed. Many non-Chinese officials enter the civil service, forcing out their Chinese counterparts.
Ming dynasty 1368–1644	The Ming restore Chinese rule to China, drive out the Mongols and bring back local officials, customs and culture. The period is generally peaceful and there is a notable flowering of the arts and crafts.
Qing dynasty 1644–1911	Non-Chinese rulers from Manchuria, the Qing cling to traditions in order to try to maintain respect for the emperor's power. At first they are successful, but they later fall prey to rebellions and to foreign powers, who gain lucrative trade concessions.
Chinese Republic 1912–1949	After the collapse of the Qing, China becomes a republic. Attempted domination by warlords is overcome by the Nationalist Party, or Kuomintang (KMT), but the KMT government is weakened by conflict with the communists and China's war with Japan.
People's Republic 1949–	After World War II, there is a civil war and the communists are victorious. Mao Zedong proclaims the People's Republic in 1949 and runs China as a totalitarian communist state. In the late twentieth century, China engages more with the capitalist economies of the West.

Left: Since the building
of the Three Gorges Dam,
this stunning gorge
scenery has changed.
Many of the cliffs have
been submerged, but the
dramatic peaks remain,
often shrouded in mist.

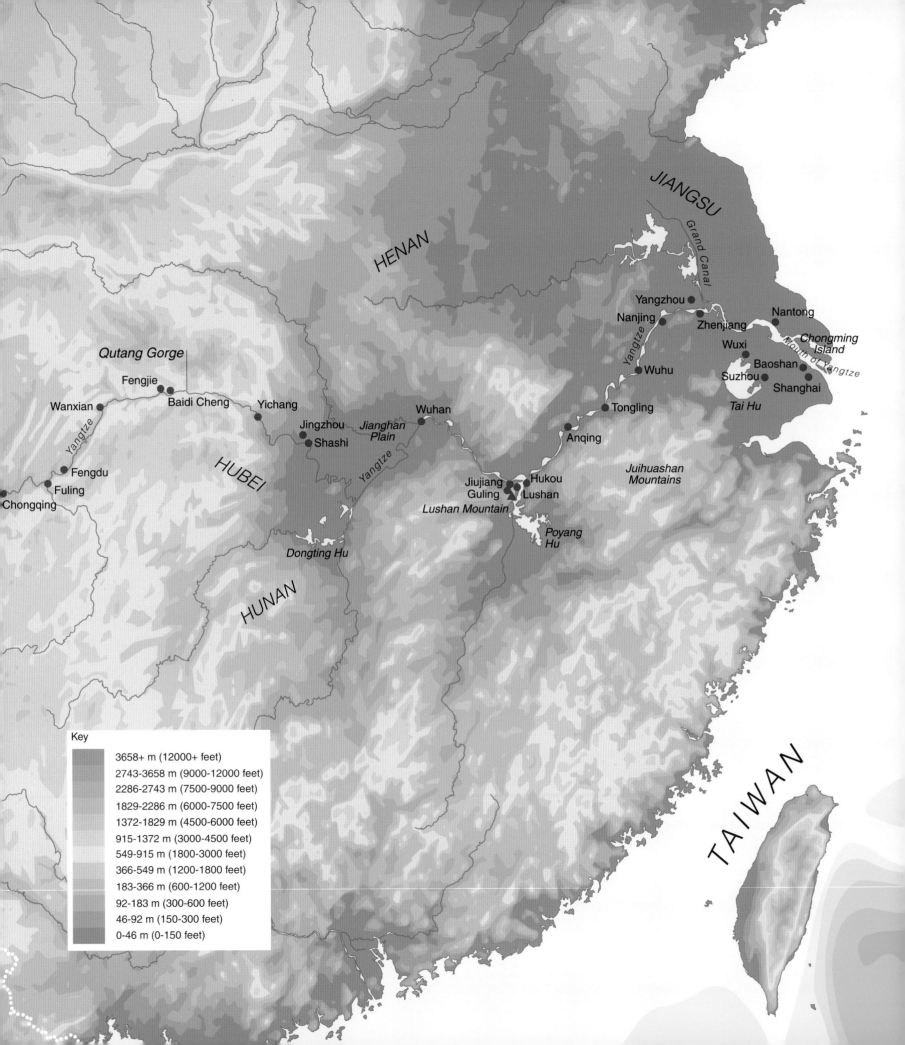

JIANGSU

HENAN

Grand Canal

Yangzhou

Nantong

Nanjing

Zhenjiang

Chongming
Island

Wuxi

Mouth of Yangtze

Qutang Gorge

Wuhu

Baoshan

Fengjie

Suzhou

Shanghai

Baidi Cheng

Yichang

Wuhan

Tongling

Tai Hu

Wanxian

Jingzhou

*Jianghan
Plain*

Yangtze

Shashi

Anqing

Yangtze

*Juihuashan
Mountains*

HUBEI

Fengdu

Jiujiang

Hukou

Fuling

Guling

Lushan

Chongqing

Lushan Mountain

*Poyang
Hu*

Dongting Hu

HUNAN

TAIWAN

Key

3658+ m (12000+ feet)

2743-3658 m (9000-12000 feet)

2286-2743 m (7500-9000 feet)

1829-2286 m (6000-7500 feet)

1372-1829 m (4500-6000 feet)

915-1372 m (3000-4500 feet)

549-915 m (1800-3000 feet)

366-549 m (1200-1800 feet)

183-366 m (600-1200 feet)

92-183 m (300-600 feet)

46-92 m (150-300 feet)

0-46 m (0-150 feet)

INTRODUCTION

The Yangtze is an eternal river. For visitors and Chinese people alike, it seems to begin in the clouds, pass across half a world of geology, wildlife and human settlement, and flow towards an endless sea. It is a journey of map-defying length. At 6300 km (3915 miles) the Yangtze is the third longest river in the world – only the Amazon and the Nile are longer. And its tumbling, snaking course from the mountains and glaciers of Tibet to the coastal region near Shanghai has more variety, more scenic richness, more diversity of people and settlement than perhaps any of the earth's great rivers. It plunges through some of the world's steepest and most dramatic rapids, squeezes between some of the tallest mountains, feeds and links some of the planet's greatest cities. It takes the Three Gorges Dam, the world's biggest at Sandouping, to hold back its waters, a Herculean task. This huge, seemingly endless, watercourse is difficult to comprehend, impossible to sum up. For the Chinese, it is simply Chang Jiang, the Long River, or sometimes, to emphasize its length still more, Wanli Chang Jiang, the Ten Thousand Li Long River.

THE COURSE OF THE RIVER

A river of the Yangtze's length passes through many different types of terrain, and through the lands of many different peoples. In its highest reaches, it passes through the homelands of people who are traditionally nomadic; many of the thinly spread population of Tibet and Qinghai still herd yaks, sheep and goats and move from place to place to find better pasture. In these cold, lonely, little-known regions, the icy country of the river's source gives way to high grasslands. Downstream, the river flows southwards along Tibet's border with Sichuan province, where the country is mountainous and the population a mix of Tibetans and Chinese.

Even here, the river has already flowed for hundreds of miles and changed its name several times. High among the glaciers it is the Tuotuo, the murmuring river. On the high Tibetan plateau it is the Tongtian, the river that travels through the heavens. Tibetans also sometimes call it the Dri Chu, or female yak river. And so the river's sound, apparently eternal course and life-force are embodied in these local names.

Further south, the river plunges into Yunnan province. This is home to several of China's minority peoples: the Naxi, who still retain a distinctive culture and language, the Bai, famous for their wood carving, and the upland Yi. The Naxi country is scenically stunning, for the Long River flows through deep rocky gorges that are the habitat of some of China's most beautiful flowers. Sights such as icy Jade Dragon Snow Mountain and plunging Tiger Leaping Gorge are among the best known on the river, although they have only recently been accessible to tourists. Here the river changes its name once more. Now it is Jinsha Jiang, the river of golden sand, for its banks are indeed sandy in some places.

After Yunnan, the river's course is generally eastwards, first of all through the region based on the port and industrial city of Chongqing, and then into Hubei province, home of the famous Three Gorges that have recently been flooded and transformed as a result of the construction of the vast Three Gorges Dam. The area was formerly the chief destination of foreign tourists, keen to join one of the many cruises and admire the steep-sided gorges. Here at last the river is commonly known by its international name of Yangtze, although since the building of the dam this stretch is now more like a vast lake than a river. But the tall mountains continue to tower over the water and the scenery still has a special, if much-changed, beauty.

The Yangtze is rich in wildlife, some of it uniquely its own. The river's most remote upper reaches are still largely undisturbed, and creatures such as wild asses and various species of deer can still be found along its banks. But in the lower reaches, pollution, over-fishing, the draining of wetlands for land reclamation, and the presence of the dam have put some of the river's creatures in danger. The Chinese sturgeon and the baiji, or Chinese river dolphin, are two of the species most at risk here.

In the lower reaches the river winds slowly, broadening appreciably as it passes through the provinces of Anhui and Jiangsu to reach its mouth at the East China Sea. This lower river passes by massive centres of population, such as the great cities of Nanjing and Shanghai, a reminder that the population of the Yangtze area is enormous – it has been estimated that almost 12 per cent of the world's population lives in the basin of the Yangtze or the 'Long River'. The lower river is also a centre of agriculture, densely packed with paddy fields where a large proportion of the country's rice – together with other crops such as silk – is grown.

In the vicinity of Shanghai and Nanjing are some of the most fertile farmlands in the world. The river, frequently bursting its banks, has spread a rich silt over the adjoining land. But this land has to be managed in order to make it viable for farming, and the history of the delta area is one of digging dykes, building flood barriers and maintaining irrigation channels. The need to keep all this going kept the Chinese far ahead of the West in water-management technology. Devices such as the waterwheel and the 'dragon's backbone', a simple treadwheel-powered pump, were in use from the first century AD for raising water.

The result of all this early land reclamation was that by the thirteenth century much of the delta was available for agriculture, and it remains intensively farmed to this day. In the resulting damp fields, farmers can grow two crops of rice per year, rotating them with wheat or soya beans to make their land trebly productive. The quantity of rice produced is staggering – the delta accounts for around one quarter of China's entire annual rice crop. Even the dykes can be pressed into service for cultivation, with sugar cane or mulberries planted on the tops. With traditional fishing taking place alongside intensive farming, all within a short distance of Shanghai's twenty-first-century commercial district, this is one of the world's greatest economic melting-pots.

THE RIVER IN HISTORY

Its waters a rich source of fish, its mud bringing fertility to the soil, its lower course a vital highway – the Yangtze has played a role in Chinese history for millennia. Some of China's earliest human remains have been found near the river. In the third century BC it was a centre for the Shu, one of the three warring peoples that gave this era the name 'Three Kingdoms period'. Great battles and the deeds of kings and generals of this time are commemorated at various points along the river. During the Tang dynasty (618–907), one of the heydays of the arts in China, many of the river's cities were cultural centres. Some of the dynasty's greatest writers, such as the poets Li Po and Tu Fu, spent time on the river and immortalized it in their works.

Another cultural flowering occurred under the Ming emperors (1368–1644). Many of the towering pagodas on the banks of the river date from this time, their colourful paintwork and curving roofs reflected in the water. Some cities also preserve their Ming defensive walls. During China's final imperial dynasty, the Qing (1644–1911), the character of the river towns changed again. Many became Treaty Ports, open for trade with foreign countries and full of overseas merchants, diplomats and soldiers. The river itself filled up with junks and sampans, as well as the vessels of the European merchants. Most elegant and striking of all were swift sailing ships such as the tea clippers, which drastically cut journey times to Europe, beginning the 'shrinking' of the world that has continued into present times.

In all these periods, the river has played its role in carrying goods and people from one part of China to another. The range of trade goods is amazing and is almost itself a portrait of China and its working life. Salt, rice, tea, rhubarb, bran, tung oil, silk, nut galls, hides, bristles – the list is endless. But the large movements along the river have mostly been in the middle and lower

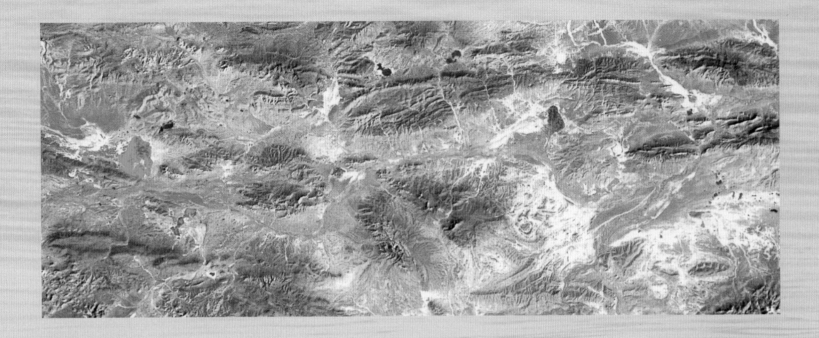

Above: Satellite images can show us a great deal about parts of the Yangtze in remote areas. This Landsat image shows the uppermost reaches, including the confluence of the Tuotuo and Dam Qu, the two rivers that have been claimed as the source waters of the Yangtze.

reaches. The upper reaches, higher than the town of Yibin above Chongqing, are not normally navigable except to small local craft, so larger boats had to stop much lower downstream. Now that the Three Gorges Dam has made the water wider and deeper, Chongqing itself has become a major port for large ships, and the trading history of the river is taking a new and still busier turn.

EXPLORING THE RIVER

The upper river, hemmed in partly by mountains, flowing elsewhere through isolated uplands, is still little known, except to those who live near its banks. This has always been the case, because, unlike many of the world's other great rivers, the Yangtze is not famous for its explorers. Westerners found it hard to travel in China before the mid-nineteenth century – the country was virtually 'closed' to outsiders. Meanwhile, local people knew their stretch of the river well. They had travelled it, fished it, farmed by it and marvelled at it for millennia, and had no need to explore. By the 1860s, however, with China increasingly open to traders and travellers from the West, Europeans began to be curious about the fascinating and fabled Long River.

The first notable explorer was Thomas Blakiston, a British soldier and traveller who was fired with the idea of bringing foreign business to the Yangtze. So in February 1861 he set off from Shanghai with a small fleet of eight hybrid sail-and-steam vessels. He and his team soon reached Hankou, where they transferred to a local junk to sail through the three gorges and on to Chongqing. By May they were in Yibin, which for most practical purposes was the highest navigable point on the river.

Blakiston's account of his journey, *Five Months on the Yang-tsze*, describes vividly the river scenery, the dolphins, the flora and the local people – as well as recounting his luck in dodging trouble in places such as Nanjing, which were then being rocked by the Taiping Rebellion.

Another British explorer, William John Gill, made his expedition in 1877. He sailed up the river to Chongqing and set up the trading post that was to become a notable Treaty Port before beginning a long overland journey through the mountains of Sichuan and Tibet. He eventually found the river again at Batang, hundreds of kilometres higher upriver than Blakiston.

But perhaps the most remarkable of all the early explorers was the British traveller Isabella Bird, who journeyed along the Yangtze in the mid-1890s. Like Gill, she set off overland after traversing the Three Gorges. Her amazing account of her travels recalls how she pushed on towards the Tibetan borders through blinding snow: 'Several times I sank in drifts up to my throat, my soaked clothes froze on me, the snow deepened, whirled, drifted, stung like pin points. But the awfulness of that lonely mountainside cannot be conveyed in words.'

Such travellers were an inspiration to the many Westerners who felt drawn to China and to the river. The next generation of travellers focused their journeys on clear practical aims. Archibald Little, for example, was a notable merchant who pioneered steam transport on the Yangtze. Little's captain, Cornell Plant, followed up this achievement by undertaking surveys of the river, collecting the results in an authoritative navigator's guide to the Yangtze between Yichang and Chongqing. Later still, explorer Joseph Rock made pioneering studies of the life of the upper river.

TAMING THE DRAGON

Westerners such as Plant and Rock have an honourable place in the story of the river, making later travellers grateful for their discoveries. In more recent times, the river has presented a different sort of challenge, with several groups vying to be the first to travel the whole of its course, rapids and all, on rafts or in sealed craft. The goal of 'running' the Yangtze – finally achieved by a Chinese team in 1986 – reflects one persistent view of the river. For many, the Yangtze is a wild creature that demands to be tamed or mastered, a great force to be overcome.

The communist leader Mao Zedong clearly felt this when he swam across the river's dangerous, snake-infested waters. And something of the same spirit lies behind the enormous project to build the Three Gorges Dam. To block the river, stop its floods and harness its power to generate electricity on a vast scale is seen as overcoming an elemental force, taming a vast dragon, as more than one commentator has put it. For now, we do not know if this process will work. The dam might tame the river. But if it bursts, or silts up irreparably, it might unleash a yet more powerful dragon, leading to unstoppable floods and uncountable deaths. The river, and China, face a turning point. But no one yet knows which way they will turn.

Below: Dragon boats, with their ornate prows, originated on the Yangtze. Now the dragon is a symbol both of the long, snaking river and of the devastating floods it has unleashed across the Chinese countryside.

CHAPTER 1

THE UPPER REACHES

For the ancient Chinese, the source of the Yangtze was in heaven. The river had such mythic power, it flowed so far, its origins were clearly so distant from the known Chinese world that the ancients felt it must have its source among the clouds. And in a way they were right. The trickle of water that becomes the Yangtze starts in a place so remote, cold and high that it might as well be in another world. It begins among the Tanggula Mountains in the border country of Tibet and Qinghai, at Mount Geladandong.

This book defines the river's upper reaches as stretching from the source to the city of Chongqing, at the confluence of the Yangtze and Jialing rivers, in the heart of China. At the far western end of this 3700-km (2300-mile) stretch, Mount Geladandong is tall and imposing at

Above: High in the Tanggula Mountains the ice slowly melts, dripping into a stream that flows between shingly banks. The Yangtze, here known as the murmuring river, is on its way.

6621 m (21,723 feet) and is about three-quarters the height of Everest. It is surrounded by glaciers that seep and drip to form the Tuotuo (or murmuring) River. Prominent among these is the Jianggudiru Glacier, which feeds a small lake called Qemo Ho, pinpointed by explorers as the source of the Yangtze. As the water trickles onwards, a network of channels and marshes comes together to join it, forming a pebbly river that flows first northwards, then eastwards through Qinghai.

It is cold and isolated here among the rocks and glaciers, and there are few people around apart from a sparse scattering of yak-herding Tibetans. Yet it is not far to Wenquan and the winding, frost-resistant road that bends its way out of China towards Lhasa. Travellers may well feel as if they are on top of the world as they journey through Wenquan, a 1950s' town that was planned as a staging-post on the Lhasa road. At 5100 m (16,732 feet) above sea level it is the highest town on earth.

The clear air and stark, imposing glaciers of Geladandong form a fitting setting for the source of one of the world's greatest rivers. But other waters have been claimed as the source of the Yangtze. The Dam Qu River, for example, joins the main Yangtze just below Tuotuo Heyan, another town on the Lhasa road, north of Wenquan. And the Qumar, which crosses the road at Qumar Heyan yet further north, joins the river still lower. Both have been suggested as sources, for, like any great river, the Yangtze has a collection of headwaters flowing into it.

In the 1970s the Chinese authorities decided to mount a scientific expedition to examine these headwaters and decide which was the river's true source. So in 1976 scientists and explorers of the Chinese Geographic Research Institute travelled the region, surveyed, studied and measured, and declared Jianggudiru Glacier and the Tuotuo to be the ultimate source of the Long River. A subsequent expedition, sponsored by the National Geographic Society in 1985, took issue with this conclusion. The Dam Qu, its surveyors insisted, is slightly longer than the Tuotuo, so has a better claim. But for most people, the sheer magnificence of the glacial scenery around Mount Geladandong sways the debate so Jianggudiru is generally accepted as the primary source – the most remote and the most dramatic, if not quite the furthest from the East China Sea.

The rocks and glaciers around Geladandong feel cold and elemental. They look as if they have hardly altered for millennia. But are they at risk in this era of climate change? There are varying theories about this. In 1999 a group of 13 Chinese women journalists made the trip to Jianggudiru to see the place at first hand. One of their number, Chen Xiaqiong, had visited the site in 1994. She noticed that the glaciers had retreated by 100 m (330 feet) in the intervening five years. 'This time we actually camped on the very site of a glacial lake I saw four years ago,' she commented. 'Now the lake [is gone], with only gravel left.' Wang Yongchen, another expedition member, recalls seeing many wild yaks, Tibetan antelope, wild Tibetan ducks and white-lipped deer when visiting the region in 1993. Now there are far fewer of these and other

wildlife species. Human activities, such as excessive grazing of domestic stock, have led to the desertification of many areas, forcing native species to move on. Wang and her colleagues have since campaigned for the protection of the area around the Yangtze headwaters.

Another friend of the area is explorer and campaigner Yang Xin, who travelled in the region between 1986 and 1994. Yang identified poaching as an activity that has led to the decline of some species. He has mounted a campaign to set up environmental protection stations in the region, where scientists, officials and volunteers have worked to develop better conservation policies and to try to curtail the poaching.

But many environmentalists are still concerned about the stability of the source waters. Recently the river levels have been low, renewing worries that the source may be drying up.

Above: The river is a lifeline for the animals that live in the upper reaches. Here a herd of yaks has come down to the water to drink.

Previous page: At the foot of Mount Geladandong the glaciers yield suddenly to grassland. From a distance the grass looks lush, but it grows between the countless stones that strew the ground in this tough country.

However, research conducted in China seems to show that the glacier area in the Geladandong area has dropped by only 1.7 per cent in the last 30 years, compared to a drop of 17 per cent in the source area of the Yellow River. Researchers argue that the glaciers around Geladandong exist at particularly low temperatures, meaning that they move very slowly and are less vulnerable to climate change than those in other regions. But the debate continues and scientists keep the ice under close scrutiny.

Murmuring marshes and golden sands

High on the plateau of Tibet and Qinghai, the windswept permafrost is criss-crossed by icy streams. It is often hard to make out the channel that begins at Geladandong, but later it gets larger, combining with other streams to make a recognizable river, that Tibetans call the Tuotuo. During the summer it is swelled by meltwater from the snowy hills around about, and the area becomes green and marshy. These are the 'murmuring marshes', where the sound of flowing water forms a continuous aural backdrop to the still dramatic upland scenery. Many animals come to eat and drink here. Travellers find it easy to spot herds of wild yaks and asses, together with flocks of geese. Rarer sights here can include groups of white-lipped deer cropping the grasses, but moving off at speed at the earliest hint of a human hunter. Rarer still are magnificent lynxes, their pointed ears alert for unwary pray.

A few miles east of the town of Tuotuo Heyan, where the river is bridged by the Qinghai–Tibet road, the Dam Qu joins the Tuotuo. In this region the river becomes known to Chinese people as the Tongtian, the river to heaven. The name is a reminder of the myth of the river's heavenly source. It is also a signal that the steep descent is beginning; the river is flowing rapidly downwards from the realm of the gods to that of mere mortals, through cascades and rapids and rocks. This is the stretch, over 800 km (500 miles) long, where skilled locals take to their flimsy-looking coracles to cross the turbulent waters. For others, the river is not safely navigable.

Above: White-lipped deer are spread widely but thinly across Tibet, Qinghai and western Sichuan. They are seen by the river in winter, when the banks offer the best source of grass and water.

To the north, the great Tanggula Mountains look down from a height of 4500 m (15,000 feet) or more. Not far on the other side of the peaks is the source of China's other great waterway, the Yellow River, which begins its own eastward journey across the northern part of this vast country. It is tough terrain, but people carve out a living here, herding yaks where there is grass and growing barley in places where the land is flat enough.

The next stretch is still longer, and heralds another name change. Still within sight of the Tanggula Mountains, the river becomes known as Jinsha Jiang, the river of golden sand, and flows at first southeast and then southwards to form the border between Tibet and the province of Sichuan. According to some, the river earned this name as the result of deposits of gold dust found along some stretches. But, more prosaically, it does indeed take on the colour of its sandy bottom in many places along this 2253-km (1400-mile) stretch of mountains, rocks and rapids. And so it continues, leaving Tibet near the isolated border town of Dege.

Above left: Buddhist monks in their plum-coloured robes gather for a prayer ceremony near the Qinghai–Sichuan border.

DEGE AND BATANG: BORDER TOWNS

Dege, on the border of the Tibet Autonomous Region, is an ancient place of pilgrimage. It is the site of two well-known monasteries of the Saskyapa order, one of the four schools of Tibetan Buddhism. Founded in 1073 at Sakya in southern Tibet, the order has been present for

Above: The river churns its way through the Chola Mountains past the wooden houses of Dege.

THE UPPER REACHES

29

Below: Clusters
of pink rhododendron
blossoms enliven the
spring scenery
of the upper reaches.

Right: Steep cliffs and
mountains force the river
into a twisting course near
Batang.

centuries at Dege, where it has built a reputation for scholarship. For 270 years Dege has been home to the Bakong Scripture Printing House, where monks and workers produce copies of the scriptures of Tibetan Buddhism.

To produce their books, the monks at Dege use printing blocks that in some cases date back to the eighteenth century. But there is nothing antique about the speed and efficiency with which the small army of workers produces the printed sheets from a collection of more than 217,000 wooden blocks. As many as 2500 sheets are printed in a single day. In this old, wooden complex there are special rooms for paper-cutting, printing and binding, which are connected by winding corridors and stairs.

As well as books, the monks also print images of the revered *bodhisattvas* of Tibetan Buddhism, the saintly beings who postpone their entry into nirvana in order to help others on the way. Most beloved of all these figures is Avalokiteshvara, the patron bodhisattva of Tibet and the embodiment of compassion. A male bodhisattva in most of the Buddhist world, Avalokiteshvara changes sex in China, to become the popular goddess of mercy, Kuan Yin.

For a long stretch north of Dege to the point among the Hengduan Mountains where it crosses into Yunnan, the river marks the border between the province of Sichuan and the Tibet Autonomous Region. For much of this stretch it is bordered by tall mountains, the Shaluli to the east in Sichuan, the Ningjing to the west in Tibet. Here the river throws up some of its most dramatic rapids. The water churns and bubbles and foams. The course of the river twists and turns through jagged rocks, plunging headlong towards the province of Yunnan. This is the part of the river that defeated the team of whitewater rafters led by American Ken Warren, who planned to negotiate the entire course of the Yangtze in 1986.

Exhausted and demoralized as a result of continuously being thrown from their rafts by the bucking current, their craft pounded and damaged, Warren's team gave up above Batang. It was left to a Chinese group to run the complete course, finishing later the same year. For their passage through the worst rapids they travelled in sealed capsules, reverting to ordinary rafts for the rest of the

journey. They lost four men but the survivors were still triumphant that a team from China had been the first to 'conquer' the country's greatest river.

The few towns among these peaks and rapids are either farming centres where the mountains give way to flatter land, or trading posts on the routes between Sichuan and Tibet. The old Tibetan town of Batang fills both of these roles. Batang is on a road between the two regions and has a mixed population of Chinese and Tibetans. A suspension bridge connects the two sides of the river but the town is not as open as this implies. The road into the town is rough, the suspension bridge is often in need of repair, and the Chinese authorities do not always open the place to visitors. Those who do make it here admire the views over farmland planted with barley towards mountains in the distance.

Below: Prayer flags flutter among the mountains above the river near Deqin. Tibetan Buddhists believe that as the flags move, the mantras written on them are 'activated' by the wind.

Right: The snow leopard is a silent predator of the uplands, rarely seen except by hunters who pursue it for its beautiful fur.

The river continues through mountains and some 40 km (25 miles) south of Batang reaches the border with the southwestern province, Yunnan. This is one of China's most beautiful and diverse provinces, home to more species of flora and fauna than any other – there are 2500 different plants alone. This is reflected in the scenery among the hills and mountains, where a vibrant palette of yellow buttercups, red poppies, white camellias, pink rhododendrons and hazy blue lavender can greet the eye. Yunnan has earned its ancient nickname, 'Kingdom of Plants'.

One of the towns nearest the border is Deqin, between the Long River and the Lancang, which runs parallel with it. So idyllic is the country around Deqin, with its flowers and mountains, that it is being hailed as the Chinese Shangri-La, allegedly the inspiration for the Buddhist paradise in James Hilton's 1933 novel *Lost Horizon*. This border country is rich in wildlife, too, and is home to the Yunnan golden monkey, snow leopard and clouded leopard.

Below: Once thought to be extinct, the Yunnan golden monkey survives in a few isolated areas of dense forest in the mountains to the south of the Yangtze.

Steep mountains and frequent snows have kept visitors away in the past, but, as with many locations along the river, this promises to change as the Chinese authorities wake up to the revenue-attracting possibilities of international tourism.

A BEND IN THE RIVER

This area is also a place to appreciate some of the finest scenery beside the Long River itself. Just over 160 km (100 miles) south of Batang, near a town called Shigu, the Yangtze performs one of its most dramatic tricks, bending back on itself in a sharp hairpin, continuing on a northern course parallel to the southern one it had followed previously.

A hill called Yun Ling (Cloud Mountain) blocks the river's way here and stops it continuing its southward course. It is not a big hill; indeed, it pales into insignificance compared with the tall Hengduan Mountains (the fabled 'horizon-splitting' range) in the middle distance. But it stands in the way of the Long River, and without it the waters of the Yangtze would flow ever southwards, away from China and down through Thailand and Cambodia, on a course similar to the Mekong. Yun Ling, the mountain that does the remarkable job of keeping the waters of the Long River in China, has, as a result, found its way into the country's myth and legend.

Right: The river bends back on itself among the mountains of Yunnan, its yellow-brown colour reminding travellers of its name in these reaches – the river of golden sand.

As so often with Chinese rivers, the story begins with a series of floods. These particular floods took place in prehistoric times, during the reign of Yao and Shun, two semi-legendary emperors who were said to have ruled some time before 2000 BC. The floods were especially bad at this time and the emperors employed a trusted official called Yu to manage new flood-control works – the usual array of lakes and drainage channels. But there was an additional requirement. Water was a precious resource, and although the emperors wanted the rivers controlled, they also wanted to keep their waters in Chinese territory.

So Yu – together, so the story goes, with a team of dragons – went to work. He carved out new river beds, filled great lakes with excess water, and even altered the courses of some of the rivers so that they would be less likely to flood. In doing so, he transformed China's physical geography. His greatest achievement was moving Yun Ling mountain so that it stood in the way of the southward course of the great Yangtze River. With the peak in its new place, the waters had to turn north again, keeping the river in China and providing the nation with its greatest waterway.

It was said that Yu devoted his whole working life to reshaping China's landscape in this way. His task was so important, and he was so devoted to it, that he was eventually chosen to be the successor to the emperor Shun. He became known as Da Yu, the great Yu, and was said to have reigned between 2255 and 2205 BC. On his death he became a popular deity and, as a figure who had saved China from destruction by flood, was one of the most revered of all the gods in the crowded pantheon of Chinese popular religion. Even in the twentieth century, he still had his devotees. Under the dominance of the Kuomintang (or Nationalist Party) (1912–49) when China was a republic, many of the traditional gods were banned and their images destroyed. Da Yu was one of the few who survived.

TO TIGER LEAPING GORGE

Now that the Yangtze's most famous gorges have been transformed by the new dam at Sandouping, lovers of Chinese scenery will really value the gorges of the upper river. Around Lijiang these are still more stunning than the famous Three Gorges used to be. For years they have been far from the edge of the tourist map, since they are hemmed in by mountains and the river is narrow here. As a result of this isolation, they were known mainly only to locals, backpackers and the more intrepid travellers. But this is about to change, as the Chinese are building better roads and promoting tourism in the area. Those who know the region lament this development, as it will transform forever a unique place of quiet beauty.

Left: Jade Dragon Snow Mountain, its summit for once clear of the usual mist, towers over everything nearby, from peaks to pagodas.

The mountains near here are high – up to 5486 m (18,000 feet) – and the river passes through deep, narrow valleys between them, the rocks often towering 3657 m (12,000 feet) above the churning water. The highest peak of all is known as Yulong Xueshan (Jade Dragon Snow Mountain), which soars to 5499 m (18,044 feet), its snowy rocks often veiled in mist. It was not until 1963 that a team of mountaineers – a group from Beijing – made it to the top of this peak, but now visitors can travel to a height of 4506 m (14,783 feet) in the chair lift that has been installed. The views of peaks and glaciers and the flat land around the town of Lijiang may be partly obscured by the mist, but they are still breathtaking.

Near Jade Dragon Snow Mountain is the most beautiful of all the Yangtze gorges, Tiger Leaping Gorge. This is probably the world's deepest river gorge, and from the water to the top of the cliffs it reaches a vertiginous 3900 m (12,800 feet) in places. The river cuts its way through the rocks for about 16 km (10 miles), and colourful flowers, such as rhododendrons and camellias, adorn the hill slopes in May and June. There is a road through the gorge now, the result of a campaign of rock-blasting, and minibuses ply this route to give visitors an easy view of the scenery. But it is still possible to walk the gorge slowly along the old narrow path, once a miners' track, doing the trip in a couple of days.

This path winds its way far above the new road, bending and doubling back on itself. It is narrow, steep and dangerous. After rain, cascades and landslips can block the track or make it fatally slippery. A number of walkers have lost their footing and plunged to their deaths in the roaring waters below. But the scenic delights are like nothing else on the river. A little more than halfway along the path is the village of Hutaoyuan (Walnut Grove), where the rocky scenery is relieved with greenery and paddy fields. This is the traditional point for travellers to break the walk, to eat, drink and sleep before tackling the slightly shorter second half of the journey, ending at the small village of Daju.

Lijiang and the Naxi

From here the river continues in a generally northerly direction before taking another dramatic change of course, this time turning south once more, back towards Jade Dragon Snow Mountain. And next to the peak is the town of Lijiang, a place that is best known as the principal home of the Naxi people, one of China's distinctive indigenous groups. The picturesque town is set amongst uplands, but it has a surrounding plain, rippled with terraces, where corn and rice are grown.

The old parts of Lijiang are refreshingly different, and one can see the isolated attraction of the place, which brought backpackers here in the 1960s and made the town a staging post on the hippie trail. Old wooden houses are crowded into tight, cobbled streets, their carved decoration a feast for the eye. A market has stalls selling local goods, which seem to struggle for space with the souvenir vendors. There are canals, too, fast-flowing channels that were originally built to bring fresh water into the town. But most of all it is the local Naxi people who make this place unlike any other. The Naxi are on average taller than the Chinese population, claim a Tibetan ancestry, and follow the indigenous Tibetan religion known as Bon. There are nearly 300,000 Naxi and most of them live in the Lijiang area. In former times they had their own distinctive way of life, and although many aspects of this have disappeared, they still keep some of their characteristic customs.

Above: Much of the country around Lijiang is farmed intensively, with stepped terraces of fields climbing these upper slopes above the river.

Right: In the Lijiang area many Naxi women still wear their traditional blue clothes. Some, especially those who belong to the Moso, a subgroup of the Naxi people, still take the leading role in family life and decision-making.

Naxi families were traditionally matriarchal. Mothers kept control of their sons through a system of love affairs called *azhu*. A young man was allowed to have a relationship with a woman from another family. He could spend the night with the girl, but in the morning he had to go back to his mother's house and work. If the young couple had children, the woman was responsible for them and they were brought up in her family. Most families were not much concerned about the paternity of their children. Goods and property were inherited by the women, and there were women elders who settled disputes between families. For all this, the Naxi stopped short of out-and-out matriarchy – the actual rulers were men.

Naxi women still wear traditional costumes – blue blouses and trousers with a blue or black apron. They also sport a cape, which has one dark side and one light side, to symbolize night and day. These capes are embroidered with seven circles, which stand for the stars. There are also two further circles, to represent the eyes of a frog, one of the ancient gods of the Naxi.

The Naxi language is interesting in two ways. To write it, the Naxi still use a script made up of pictographs, tiny images of recognizable objects. The language also carries with it evidence of the matriarchal Naxi ethos. A feminine addition to a noun in Naxi indicates that the object is

larger. So the word for 'stone' plus a feminine element means 'boulder'. The opposite is also true – 'stone' plus a masculine element translates as 'pebble'.

Like all indigenous peoples, the Naxi have spent generations adapting to their local environment. One of the key skills they have developed is in building. Their wooden structures are ideally suited to the area, where earthquakes are common. There was a major quake in 1996, in which some 300 people lost their lives and many of Lijiang's modern concrete buildings were destroyed. The traditional Naxi houses fared far better, and much of the town has now been rebuilt along traditional lines. By 1999 the town was thriving again, and UNESCO declared Lijiang county a World Heritage Site. This status in turn draws more visitors to the town, as the Chinese open up this part of Yunnan and attract increasing numbers of tourists to this very special scenic region.

JOSEPH ROCK

One Western name closely associated with Lijiang and the Long River is that of the American traveller, naturalist and ethnographer Joseph Rock. Rock spent most of the years from 1922 until 1949 in Asia, and for much of this time he was based near the river at Lijiang. From here he went on a series of expeditions in China – notably in Yunnan, Sichuan and Gansu, but also in Tibet, Burma, Cambodia and Vietnam. Using funds supplied by a variety of American organizations, including Harvard University, the National Geographic Society and the US Department of Agriculture, he collected thousands of plant and animal specimens. He also made maps of these areas, which were hardly known at all in the West. And he studied local peoples, particularly the Naxi, about whom he wrote extensively, learning their language and recording their customs.

Rock vastly increased Western knowledge of southwestern China. He put thousands of plants on record for the first time, and exported species that were well suited to conditions in the West, thereby leaving a

Below: On his expeditions in and around Lijiang, Joseph Rock collected and photographed a wealth of information about local people, lifestyles, arts and crafts.

lasting legacy in the parks and gardens of Europe and North America. He is remembered by gardeners in the botanical names of several plants, such as *Rhododendron rockii*, by anthropologists for his monumental work *The Ancient Nakhi Kingdom of Southwest China*, and by readers of the *National Geographic Magazine,* who still marvel at his photographs of precipitous peaks, teetering wooden villages and swaying suspension bridges.

THE LONG MARCH

From the country around Lijiang that Joseph Rock so loved and admired, the river zigzags its way generally eastwards and then northeastwards. For some 480 km (300 miles) of this northeastward zigzag it forms the border between the provinces of Yunnan and Sichuan. Not far east of Lijiang is the industrial city of Panzhihua, a busy steel-producing city with factories built during Chairman Mao's 'Great Leap Forward', the disastrous adventure into ill-planned industry and intensive agriculture of 1958–61. This policy involved poorly organized factories, backyard blast-furnaces producing worthless steel to unrealistic quotas, and the attempt to abolish money and private property. Worse still, the switch to intensive agricultural methods did not work and caused a massive famine in which millions died. Panzhihua is a monument to the dark side of Chinese industry, something for which Mao would not have wanted to be remembered. But a short distance further upstream lies Jiaopingdu, which played its role in one of the communist leader's greatest triumphs.

In the late 1920s and early 1930s, Chinese politics were dominated by a struggle between the Nationalist Party and the communists. The nationalists held sway in the east, governing the country from Beijing; local warlords controlled the remainder of the country. The communists, under the influence of the young activist Mao Zedong, were gaining strength in many rural areas. By 1930 they had amassed a large army and were defending themselves well against attacks by the nationalists, under their leader Chiang Kai-shek. But in 1933 and 1934 the tide began to turn, and the nationalists inflicted a number of severe defeats on the communists – partly because the latter had changed their tactics and, against Mao's wishes, had met their enemies in a series of pitched battles.

By 1934 the communists' only stronghold was in the province of Jiangxi, where they had set up a small communist state, the Jiangxi Soviet. Here, among the mountains of the Jiangxi–Hunan borders, they persuaded the peasants to join them in defeating the local landlords and portioning out

Below: A memorial to Mao's Long March and those who helped him cross the river stands within sight of the waters that posed such a barrier for anyone who wanted to cross China from the south to the north.

the land between the workers. The Chinese Communist Party's Central Committee, who were no longer safe in Shanghai, also joined them here.

But they were vulnerable because the nationalists' vast army could surround them, trapping them in the mountains, which they did in October 1934. To many, the communists seemed doomed, but a few of the leaders hatched a desperate plan. They would break out of Jiangxi and march across country, moving northwards to join up eventually with other communist forces in Shaanxi. And so the famous Long March had begun.

Around 80,000 communists left Jiangxi. They were marching through difficult country, and had to fight much of the way, as they were pursued by nationalist forces. Many thousands had already been lost – to sickness, fatigue and desertion, as well as nationalist attacks – by the time they reached the Yangtze at Jiaopingdu in April 1935. Mao's scouts arrived ahead of the main columns of marchers. They thought that Jiaopingdu was a good bet as a crossing place because it was on a major

Above: A group of Long Marchers in Jiangxi look well equipped and optimistic. They needed all the courage and strength they could summon to complete their extraordinary journey.

Opposite: Fields of rice sustain the local population in Sichuan, and many outside the province also benefit from its productivity. Every available space is used for cultivation.

north–south trade route into the province of Sichuan and towards Shaanxi and the old capital of China, Xi'an. So there would be boats here, and the marchers could ferry themselves across. The place also has high cliffs, making it difficult to attack from the air.

The scouts duly dealt with the small nationalist guard at Jiaopingdu and commandeered a few small boats. Gradually, over a period of nine days, the boats shuttled backwards and forwards, ferrying the marchers – by then perhaps 45,000 of them, to the other side of the Yangtze. Here Mao and his fellow leaders set up their headquarters for a while in caves above the river. Among their number were several who were to take key positions in the communist governments of the post-war years – Mao himself, Zhou Enlai, Lin Biao and even the young Deng Xiaoping. So the shape of China's future was discussed here, near the banks of the Long River, in the middle of the communists' epic retreat.

By October 1935 the survivors of the march at last reached the city of Yan'an in central Shaanxi, where they also set up home in caves and brought the local peasants round to their cause. It was 9655 km (6000 miles) from their starting point. Only about 8000 of the original

marchers made it all the way to Shaanxi, together with another 20,000 or so who joined as new recruits along the way. But they had proved that their organization could stick together, that they could win over people in rural areas, that they could cross formidable barriers like the mountains and the Long River itself, and that they could be inspired by the leadership of Mao, Zhou and their colleagues. And so this great adventure was soon viewed as a triumph for the communists and a turning point in China's history.

TOWARDS THE SICHUAN BASIN

One group who became allies of the communists during this period was the Yi, an indigenous people who live among the mountains of northeastern Yunnan and southeastern Sichuan. There are some 5.5 million Yi, and the Yangtze River makes its way past their homes as it threads its way east and north away from Yunnan, through the Sichuan hills that are now part

of the large administrative area centred on the burgeoning city of Chongqing. The river is gradually getting wider here, but is still under 30 m (100 feet) across in most places. There are churning rapids and a mixture of muddy banks and rocky cliffs. Mountains tower above on either side.

One of the main towns on this stretch is Yibin, famous as the place where the Min River joins the Long River, which above Yibin is still known as the Jinsha Jiang, the river of golden sand. Yibin, therefore, can claim to be the place where the great Yangtze proper begins. Among the mountains around Yibin is a bamboo forest and many orange groves, forming a pleasant and productive backdrop to what is now a city of some 600,000 people. It is known as a place of industry and commerce, where road, rail and air routes meet – as well as traffic on the river, for here, at last, the waters are navigable. So there are plenty of boats, together with logs for the timber trade, which are floated from far upriver, and are collected together into rafts to make their onward journey downstream. As for industry, Yibin is where a famous Chinese spirit, known as Five Cereals Liquid, has been distilled for centuries.

It is not only the Min that joins the Long River in this region. The Jialing flows from the north, meeting the Yangtze at Chongqing, while the Wujiang joins it from the south, much farther downstream at Fuling. So hereabouts there are four major rivers – and 'four rivers' is the original meaning of the name 'Sichuan'. The flat lands around the rivers and to the north form the Sichuan Basin, a vital area for China because fertile soil, mild winters and a good rainy season make it good farmland. Grain, cotton, silk and hemp have been grown here and exported into many parts of China for centuries. One of the most important cities, in the heart of this confluence of waters, is Chongqing.

CHONGQING: A CITY ON THE MOVE

The major city of Chongqing is known as a place of mountains, rivers and fog. Its streets rise on cliffs above the Yangtze and Jialing rivers towards the mountains, often shrouded in mist, beyond. The traditional scene was one of rather rickety wooden houses apparently climbing the steep cliffs, packed tightly together with just enough space for residents to sit outside and enjoy the cool of a summer night.

It has always been an important place. As early as two million years ago there were humans here. Their stone tools were dug up by archaeologists in 1996, pushing back the arrival of humans in the area around a million years. By the fourth century BC there was a city here and it was the capital of the state of Ba. The first emperor, who united China in the third century BC made it the headquarters of the Ba prefecture. The place won its name, which means 'double celebration', in 1189, when the Southern Song emperor Zhaodun, who was born here, came to the throne.

Already, Chongqing was a key trading centre for goods coming in along the Yangtze and its local tributaries. Salt and silk, copper and iron, furs and skins – all were bought and sold here. In the late nineteenth century, foreign powers exploited the city's key position and Chongqing was opened to foreign trade. European steamboats made the perilous journey through the Three Gorges and docked here, bringing great wealth to Chongqing. But many of the city's facilities were still basic, and all Chongqing's water had to be carried up from the river by hand.

By 1939 the place was big and bustling. The combination of good communications and relative remoteness made it attractive to the Nationalist government during their war with Japan in the 1930s. So when the capital at Nanjing was destroyed by the Japanese, Chongqing became

the capital of China. It was a difficult time, when squadrons of Japanese bombers flew in and obliterated whole areas of Chinese cities. But Chongqing was better defended than most – not just by its mountainous setting, but by its frequent fogs, which caused numerous Japanese raids to go off course and miss their targets.

Above: Wooden-framed buildings, stilted high on poles to avoid flood waters, can be seen in the old city of Chongqing.

Winter fogs protected the city, but in the summers the Japanese bombers came in waves, often five or six times a day, occasionally as often as twenty times. Many lost their lives, but those who could took to shelters carved into the rock of the cliffs on which the city stands. Even in these man-made caves, people were at risk. Some died of heat exhaustion, others, relying on shelters that had been dug in earth rather than solid rock, perished when the roofs caved in. The city was scarred, but it survived.

Now Chongqing is a city on the move. At the upstream end of the vast reservoir created by the Three Gorges Dam it is being transformed. For the first time, really large ships can sail all the way up the Yangtze to Chongqing, and the place is becoming a major port. The government has planned for this by giving the place national status – in other words, it has become a metropolitan region on a par with Beijing and Shanghai. Its administrative region is home to more than 30 million people, and the river is bringing in many of their supplies. The city has always been a distribution centre for Sichuan province – now this role is growing at speed.

So Chongqing is changing in order to cope with this new status and new business. Barges heavy with goods arrive in their hundreds. Countless porters, known collectively as the *bang bang jun* (help army), carry the goods up the staircases from the docks to the city. Lorries charge along the wide roads built above the new river walls. Not surprisingly, Chongqing, frantic with commercial energy, has the worst air pollution in China.

If the Chinese authorities are right, all this is set to continue when the Three Gorges Dam is generating electricity at full strength. Cheap power and increased trade will boost Chongqing's economy and the place will grow and prosper. For the 30 million people of its municipal area it will be an evermore important centre. It will, that is, if things go according to plan. An alternative scenario, feared by many scientists is that the dam will silt up and the river will have no outlet for the million of tons of sewage dumped in it every year.

In the meantime, Chongqing is a busy working city. New retail malls and residential blocks appear on the skyline, many covered with flashing advertising signs that seem to belie China's communist heritage. The place is a paradise for consumers, eager to part with their money in the latest shops and restaurants. At nights the illuminated signs and countless cars make Chongqing a city of animated lights, one of the glinting symbols of the new, twenty-first century China. But the shining cars also bring traffic jams and pollution, its effects made worse by the city's humid climate. Like every big Western city – and more and more cities in China – Chongqing embraces both the excitement and the risks that come with change.

THE UPPER REACHES

CHAPTER 2

THE THREE GORGES

Daba Mountains

New Wushan
Wushan

Daning

Shennu Feng
(Goddess Peak)

Qutang Gorge
Guandukou

Xiling Gorge

Fengjie
Old
Zigui

Three
Gorges
Dam

New Fengjie

Daixi
Peishi
Badong

Wu Gorge
Sandouping

New Zigui

Wanxian
Gezhouba Dam

HUBEI

Yangtze
Yichang

Fengdu

Fuling

HUNAN

Chongqing

CHONGQING

Wu River

Ever since people have sailed on the Yangtze, they have watched the water level with obsessive care – and nowhere more so than in the river's most famous stretch, the series of stunning, mountain-flanked reaches known as the Three Gorges between the old city of Fengjie and Yichang, about 200 km (125 miles) downstream. In years gone by, boatmen watched the level because they knew that beneath the surface lurked jagged rocks that could wreck their craft. For those on the banks, there was the added anxiety caused by flooding. Today, everyone from engineers to farm workers scrutinizes the behaviour of the Yangtze for a different reason – to gauge the effect of the new Three Gorges Dam, the biggest civil engineering project in the world.

At Fuling, on the stretch of the river between Chongqing and the gorges, the locals began to mark the water level at least as far back as the Tang dynasty. They created a water-level scale in the form of fourteen fish carved on the rocks. The fish, which were visible only at low water,

Above: At Fuling carved fish were revealed as the water level in the river fell. Devices like this gave boatmen and townspeople a simple indication of the height of the river and the likelihood of flooding. With the construction of the dam, the fish have disappeared for good.

were eagerly watched by the region's farmers, for, according to an old saying, 'Stone fish appear, good harvest here'. With the dam in operation, the water will never again drop low enough to reveal the original stone fish, although new ones are being carved higher up the rocks.

This stretch of the river is a busy highway. Upstream passengers know they are nearing the major port of Chongqing; those going downstream are looking forward to the breathtaking scenery of the gorges. The area is steeped in history. Fengdu, for example, was known as the 'city of ghosts', and boatmen would moor only in midstream for fear the spectres would sally out from the town and attack them. The town's strange nickname probably began with a misunderstanding. During the Han dynasty, two Taoist sages called Yin and Wang lived here. When you put their names together you get the Chinese phrase meaning 'King of the Underworld'. Ever since, the superstitious have trembled as they passed.

A more welcoming sight is one of the river's most beautiful buildings, Shibaozhai (Precious Stone Fortress). This eyecatching structure has a twelve-storey pavilion built against the rocks beside the river. With its glowing red walls, gold-rimmed round windows and upturned roofs, it

is now isolated, the waters of the risen river swirling around it. This extraordinary tapering tower looks like something from another world, and above its gate, decorated with lions and dragons, is an inscription welcoming the visitor to fairyland. For the local people of Shibaozhai, it is another story. Relocated to a new, higher village to escape the rising water, they face a different, twenty-first-century reality.

Many of the people of Wanxian, the big city about two hours upriver, have had the same fate. About two-thirds of the population has had to move. Famous sights, such as the great stairways leading up from the river to the city, and the old market selling local products such as rattan and bamboo, are now submerged. Smaller settlements above the gorges, such as the market town of Fengjie, have also been affected.

ENTERING THE GORGES

For centuries the city of Fengjie had a sense of expectation about it, for it is the last town before the gorges, and all travellers down the river knew that they were on the brink of a memorable journey. Until the coming of the dam, Fengjie still boasted part of its ancient wall, built in the

Opposite: The pavilion of Shibaozhai is one of the river's most stunning structures. A special barrier is being built to protect it from the new high water level.

fifteenth century during the Ming dynasty. A long flight of stone steps led from the river bank to the main southern gate in the old wall. This, the apartment blocks around the gate, many traditional whitewashed houses of the old city and markets selling fruit, vegetables, and herbs have all disappeared since the water levels began to rise. But peaches, tangerines and oranges are still among the fruit grown in the area, and local markets have a welcoming glow during the autumn orange season. People still pause here, relaxing over tea and admiring the view downriver towards the gorges.

Travellers still feel a thrill of anticipation at the approach to the gorges, for if the steep limestone cliffs are submerged, the mountains are still imposing, reflected in the spreading waters of the river. As the swelling Yangtze finds its new course through the rocks, it makes its way past peak after peak, the rocks folding away into the distance until they disappear into the mist.

People have been moved by this scene for centuries. One of the first to record his impressions was the great Tang dynasty poet Li Po (701–762). In one of his most famous lyrics, he evoked the atmosphere of a downstream journey as his boat approached the entrance to the Qutang Gorge and made its way down towards Jiangling. The layer upon layer of mountains, the mists and the surging current pushing the boat on its way all captured his imagination:

> *Off at dawn through coloured clouds from White King City.*
> *Downstream to Jiangling we do a thousand li a day!*
> *Monkeys cling to the cliffs, no end to their screeching.*
> *Ten thousand folded mountains our boat passes on its way.*

White King, or White Emperor, City is Baidi Cheng, on the river's northern bank just above the gorges. 'City' is a misnomer. Baidi Cheng is little more than a walled village perched high above the water, with views down to the river and Qutang Gorge. But it is a place steeped in history. As Li Po passed it, he would have been aware more than anything else of those 'folded mountains' and how the 'coloured clouds' of mist seemed to wrap them in legend.

One old story tells of Gong Sunshu, an ambitious soldier and former official who lived in the first century, some 700 years before Li Po made his journey. The legend recalls how Gong Sunshu saw a cloud of mist, apparently rising from a well. The mist wound and curled until, to Gong's

Above: Food markets, selling everything from herbs and spices to tomatoes and chillies, are familiar among the winding streets of the old riverside cities. This one is in Wanxian, but there are similar ones all over China. Many of those by the Yangtze have been moved uphill and away from the rising waters of the new reservoir.

Previous page: Although they look harsh and barren from a distance, the upper parts of the limestone cliffs of Qutang Gorge are home to a variety of scrubby plants.

THE THREE GORGES

amazement, it took the shape of a dragon. In China a dragon is seen as an omen of good fortune and Gong took it as a sign that if he aimed high he would realize his ambitions. So he declared himself White Emperor, and ruled peacefully for twelve years.

The locals built a temple to mark the White Emperor's reign, and anyone willing and able to climb the steps through the woods up Baidi Mountain can still visit it. The temple is much changed now, for it was rebuilt during the Ming dynasty, when Gong Sunshu's statue was

Above: The distinctive shapes of the peaks above Qutang Gorge will remain, however high the water is allowed to rise.

removed and replaced with those of several later heroes. But it is still an evocative place and the views are magnificent, for from here the worshipper can see clearly the entrance to the first of the gorges. With the coming of the Three Gorges Dam, the landscape here has been transformed and Baidi Mountain has become an island.

Back at river level, the approach to Qutang, the first of the celebrated Three Gorges, is dramatic, with its sheer, looming peaks. It was also formerly hazardous because there were low rocks shelving out into the stream. The old riverboat captains knew that these rocks spelt danger and they kept a constant watch as they rode the rapid current. Worst of all was Yanyu Rock, a notorious obstacle some 20 m (65 feet) wide and twice as high, that threatened to wreck their vessels. Everyone knew at least one ship that had perished there, and a good boatman prided himself that he could predict what the dangers were by the water level around the rock.

The place developed a folklore of its own, and the more poetic boatmen compared the rock to different animals as its appearance altered with the water level. When the water was low, the rock loomed like a great grey elephant; at higher flood levels, Yanyu looked more like a horse. Such whimsical comparisons evolved into river proverbs, and one boatman would advise another: 'Yanyu's a horse, avoid the downstream course. Elephant Yanyu, upstream's taboo.' Whatever it looked like, the rock was a problem and a challenge. Captains celebrated the day in 1959 when a team of demolition workers arrived, armed to the teeth with high explosives. It took them a week to blast the rock away. Now the river has risen, ships sail by easily, their passengers unaware of this historic hazard.

As you pass Baidi Cheng and the site of the old Yanyu Rock, there seems to be no way through: steep cliffs block the way ahead. Then the river makes a sharp right-hand turn and, framed by the sheer cliffs of two precipitous mountains, the entrance to the gorge, Kui Men, is revealed. Here the passage through the Three Gorges begins.

A PERILOUS PASSAGE

Qutang is the shortest of the Three Gorges, but the most breathtaking. The cliffs here are the sheerest, the rocks the most 'folded' and the mountains the tallest – the limestone peaks either side tower to almost 1219 m (4000 feet) in some places. Although the two mountains of Kui Men are both made of the same rock, they look very different because of the differing chemical

deposits on either side of the gorge. On the southern bank is White Salt Mountain, so called because of the pale calcium deposits on its rocks. It faces Red Armour Mountain, which gets its colour from deposits of iron oxide. But the names of the mountains tell only part of the story of these rocks' rich colour palette. To the red and white are added a range of yellows and browns, as well as the rich dark green of plant growth where the sheer cliffs give way to gentler slopes. Changing with the light of the sun from hour to hour and day to day, Qutang Gorge boasts some of the Yangtze's most colourful scenery.

At times of high water the river's level could rise at staggering speed here, increasing as much as 49 m (160 feet) or more from one season to the next. Boatmen recall stories of how the river used to build up like a trough, with deep, surging water in the middle of the channel and high waves lashing the cliffs on either side. Another famous Tang dynasty poet, Du Fu, described the waters churning this way and that as 'fighting for the gate at Qutang'. No wise captain would expose his craft to the lashing such waters could give or risk wrecking it on the rocks.

Above: The reservoir slowly engulfs Li Duanhao's famous inscription on the riverside cliff. Many of these historic inscriptions are being recarved higher up the rock face, as memorials to their original creators.

Even when the waters were low, the upstream passage was well-nigh impossible against the mighty current so loaded junks had to be hauled up the river by some of its most famous workers, the Yangtze trackers. Large boats would carry a number of men who were strong enough to do this tiring work. But on difficult stretches of the river they would be joined by local specialists, to provide the extra power needed to work with the perilous currents. Although they sometimes worked in the water, the trackers also had a towpath, on the northern bank. It took the form of a low slot or gallery cut into the face of the cliff, just high and wide enough for the trackers to do their work of pulling along the boats by means of tough hawsers made of strips of woven bamboo.

The towpath looked high, but it had to be. Until the late nineteenth century there was a lower path, but at high water it was submerged and useless. Boats got stranded and passengers had to make a hard and tedious trek through the peaks to reach their destination or rejoin the river higher up. So in 1889 the local people set to and carved out a higher path, allowing trackers to work when the water rose.

At both low water and high, a tracker put his life on the line every time he worked. One false move by his team – or by the pilot steering the boat – could flip him off the cliff and down to an

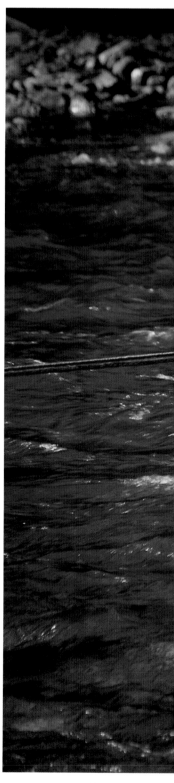

THE THREE GORGES

Opposite: A twenty-first century traveller makes his way carefully along one of the trackers' paths. Even before the dam, this walkway was often submerged.

Below: For the benefit of modern tourists, a group of trackers, stripped for action, hauls a vessel through a shallow stretch of the river.

uncertain fate among the rocks and waters below. The Victorian traveller Isabella Bird recalled how 'Many fall over the cliffs and are drowned; others break their limbs and are left on shore to take their chance – and a poor one it is – without splints or treatment…' She noticed that most trackers' bodies were covered with cuts, bruises, wounds, weals and similar marks of their dangerous work.

CHAINS AND BELLOWS

If Qutang Gorge was perilous to travellers and trackers, its narrow course offered a unique opportunity to imperial China's soldiers and generals. Because the river was so narrow, it was possible to control the traffic along it, and this proved important in times of war, when Kui Men became the ideal place to hold up enemy shipping. Probably the first to take full advantage of this were the rulers of the Tang dynasty and the kings of the Five Dynasties that succeeded the Tang in the tenth century. One chronicle tells how the King of Shu commissioned his commander Zhang Wu to guard the gorges. One day in AD 925 a rival from Jingzhou, the self-styled king of Nanping (northern Sichuan), sailed up the river to try to take some of Shu's lands. Zhang Wu strung iron chains across the river, preventing the Nanping fleet from sailing through. Then the wind got up, the Nanping boats began to get tangled in the chains, and were unable to move. Zhang Wu ordered his men to hurl rocks from the cliffs and the enemy craft were sunk.

Some time after this triumph, two iron posts were set in rocks in the river bed to make it easier to string the chains across. From then on, the imperial authorities had full control over the traffic through the gorges. Not only could they stop their enemies, they could also use the chains as a sort of customs barrier. Craft sailing downriver could be stopped, charged a duty and sent on their way. This system was so successful that the local tax office at Fengjie county became one of the richest in the whole of China. So the emperors had the chains strengthened and the tax-collecting carried on well into the Qing dynasty. Before the construction of the Three Gorges Dam, the pillars that supported the chains could still be seen when the water in the river was low.

On the south side of the river, up the side of the mountain Baiyan Shan, a number of ancient cuts in the rock, now submerged, are being recarved higher up. They make a series of holes, apparently footholds, rising halfway up the cliff. Why only halfway? A legend supplies one answer. It is said that during the Song dynasty a famous general, Yang Jiye, was buried

Left: A passenger boat snakes its ways through a quiet Qutang Gorge. With the coming of the dam, and the higher, deeper waters it brings with it, much bigger vessels are becoming a familiar sight in these reaches of the river.

on a high terrace on the mountain. One of his most loyal men, Meng Liang, decided that he would take the general's bones back to his home town for a proper burial. It was a task that had to be carried out secretly at night. One night Meng Liang began to cut a stairway up the rock to reach the terrace, but could not finish it because he was spotted by a monk who started crowing like a cock. Thinking morning was near, Meng Liang retreated; when he discovered the trick, he hanged the monk upside down from a nearby crag. The crag is now called Daodiao Heshangshi (Hanging Monk Rock).

There is another simpler explanation for this stairway that seems to lead nowhere up the rock face. It is thought that it was carved into the rock by people who wanted to gather medicinal

herbs. For then as now, traditional Chinese medicine relied on a variety of natural remedies, some based on rare plants that grow in places that are hard to reach. Even so, the power of the ancient legend is such that the flight of footholds is still called Meng Liang Stairway.

Opposite the stairway is a series of holes that took wooden beams to support several wooden boxes. These boxes reminded people of the bellows used by Chinese blacksmiths, so this part of Qutang became known as Fengxiang Xia (Bellows Gorge). One local legend said that the boxes were part of a bellows used by the god Lu Ban. In fact the boxes are coffins, for some locals found a final resting place high on the riverside cliffs. They were members of the Ba tribe, a people who lived in the region during the Warring States period, so their cypress-wood coffins have worn very well. Some, hung vertically, apparently inspiring a poem by Meng Chiao:

Trees lock their roots in rotted coffins
And the twisted skeletons hang tilted upright.

Even here, among the stunningly beautiful rock faces, their colours ranging from pale white through pink to purple, and amid the delicately branched trees, that cling to their crevices, the passer-by is reminded of death and danger.

KILLING THE DRAGON AND ENDING THE FLOOD

The town of Daixi stands at the downstream end of Qutang Gorge. Daixi is known mainly to archaeologists, since it is a site where more than 200 Stone Age burial sites have been found, complete with grave goods made of stone, bone and jade. Here, beyond the famed gorge, the scenery is still beautiful. A few miles downstream from Daixi a pair of dark, jagged mountains frame the river, forming one of the Yangtze's many smaller gorges. This one is known as Suokai Xia (Unlocked Gates Gorge) and it was famed for two rocks – one shaped like a pillar, the other like a drum – on opposite banks.

The names of these two rocks, Suolong Zhu (Binding Dragon Pillar) and Zhanglong Tai (Beheading Dragon Platform) reminded passers-by that they are steeped in legend. The story goes that there was once a dragon who lived up the Daixi Stream, a small tributary that joins the river near Daixi. The dragon lost its way when it ventured on to the Yangtze to visit its relatives and a local boy made matters worse by giving it misleading directions. The dragon was so angry that it hurled itself against the mountains, causing a mighty landslide that blocked the

river. There was a flood, people and their animals were killed, and many houses and farms were destroyed. The survivors were saved by the goddess Yao Ji, who bound the dragon to the stone pillar. The dragon showed no sign of remorse for what it did, so the goddess called on another deity, the god Da Yu, who was famous for his ability to control floods. Da Yu took the dragon across to the stone platform on the opposite bank of the river and beheaded it. Da Yu then cut a new channel for the river so that the people of the area could once more resume their lives in safety.

Tales like this show how early peoples explained the capricious nature of the river, where floods could destroy a season's harvest or, worse still, wipe out whole communities. Such stories often feature Da Yu, the god whose power over the floods and whose work draining the land made farming possible in China. Such myths show respect for the strength of the river and for the power of forces that were quite beyond ordinary people's control. They remind us that farming was vital for the people's survival and that in many places navigable rivers were the main transport routes.

Above: This old print shows Da Yu, who was said to have been born into an ordinary lower-class family, rising through the civil service to become emperor. When he died he joined the gods, and his work in saving China from floods has meant he has always been a popular deity.

Opposite: Distinctive sloping hills, rising more gradually than at Qutang, mark the entrance to Wu, the second of the famous Three Gorges.

WUSHAN

Da Yu is also a presence in Wushan, the town at the entrance to the second of the three great gorges. Wushan was an old town, site of a palace of the king of Chu during the Warring States period. Later it was a centre of Buddhism, with many temples and shrines. Most of these have long disappeared, but there is still a temple to Yao Ji and Da Yu on Gaoqiu Mountain nearby. Today the old city has been demolished and the water has risen to cover its site. The old streets with their courtyard houses and markets have vanished and a new Wushan has been built, three times the size of the original town. As well as the inhabitants of the original Wushan, many people from smaller settlements on the river banks have moved here to start a new life.

Looking at the area today, it is still easy to understand why Buddhist monks were keen to settle here. The town is beautifully set among the hills above the river, and the area is well provided with natural resources. Foremost of these is the tung or tallow tree that grows in the region. This is an oil-bearing tree, and the oil was used widely by the river people for varnishing and caulking their boats. Visitors still look out for the tallow trees, marvelling at their changing beauty. In spring and summer their grey trunks are complemented by lush green leaves. The leaves turn a rich red in the autumn, and in winter there are the striking white seeds to be seen.

Left: Small houses clustering at the foot of the cliffs near Wushan are relics of a traditional riverside life that is disappearing with the coming of the dam.

At Wushan the Daning River joins the Yangtze. The Daning hereabouts is like a small cousin of the Yangtze, with its own trio of small gorges. The so-called Little Three Gorges have their own character, quieter and more remote than the Yangtze gorges. The river water is clear, the vegetation in many places is lush and green, and with the flooding of the Three Gorges, visitors come here to experience the dramatic scenery of the river's hinterland. They may also catch a glimpse of the river's wildlife: hunting golden eagles soar among the uplands; flying squirrels glide from tree to tree; mandarin ducks whistle eerily as they fly from their tree-hole nests to the waters of local streams or lakes. Understandably, more and more tourists take a trip up the Little Three Gorges and back, and the Daning region is making a worthwhile contribution to the area's tourism industry which could have declined severely with the construction of the dam.

WU GORGE – MISTY PEAKS

Wu Gorge is celebrated for its beauty. Here the Yangtze works its way through the Wushan Mountains, and the river traveller is treated to an ever-changing vista of peaks as the water

Left: The golden eagle, soaring above the river and its peaks, will keep its high, mountain-top eyries in spite of the rising waters below.

stretches first this way, then that. In places the mountains bare their rocks, but in other spots they are green and lush, and in spring the area can be alive with leaves and blossom. The gorge is also a place of mists, which often come down to shroud the tops of the peaks, lending the scenery an air of mystery. But here and there the mists will lift, revealing more trees and bushes. Wu Gorge – the name means Witches' Gorge – is indeed a place of magical transformations.

Below: The elegant mandarin duck is a familiar sight on China's waterways.

The magic inspired the locals to poetic metaphor and simile like no other place on the river. About 10km (6 miles) downstream from Wushan one comes upon a notable example of this. On one bank of the river is a striking off-white-coloured layered rock formation that has long been dubbed Silver Armour Rock because it is said to resemble the shining armour once worn by Chinese warriors. Nearby is Golden Helmet Rock, so called because its shape and colour recall a soldier's helmet. These are just two examples of the folk poetry that surrounds the river, creating memorable myths and phrases out of the local scenery. But there are many more.

Twelve peaks overlook this stretch of the river and they are surrounded by legend. They all have picturesque names that refer to their appearance (Shangsheng Feng – Mounting Aloft Peak) or their climate (Cuiping Feng – Misty Screen Peak). These mountains, with their striking profiles and

ever-changing scenery, are the legacy of the area's climate and geology. In the rainy season of July and August the area is often stormy, and millennia of rain have sculpted the local soft limestone into jagged outlines. The resulting shapes of the mountains have inspired countless poets and painters, and the peaks have been compared to the scales of a fish, the horns of cattle, birds in flight, or crowds of people watching over the river.

The best known of all these mountains is Shennu Feng, Goddess Peak, which, as its name suggests, is shrouded in myth as well as mist. Shennu Feng is a tall twin summit that towers above the neighbouring crags. To past observers its shape suggested a young woman kneeling reverently before a pillar, and they decided that the peak was Yao Ji, the goddess who saved the river people from floods by binding a dragon to a rock near Daixi. The story of Yao Ji is ancient and has been handed down through the generations in different ways. In some versions, there were twelve dragons causing mayhem around the river: Yao Ji tamed them all and turned them into the twelve peaks that line the gorge. In another variation, Yao Ji stayed on to protect the gorge. She and her eleven handmaidens became the twelve mountains that look benevolently over the river and protect the locals from storms and floods. Some say their power extends much further, and that they look after the river people's crops and help to heal the sick. The legends constantly alter in the retelling, like the twisting, changing course of the river itself.

The mists of Wu Gorge are famous, but it would be wrong to portray this stretch of the river as forever shrouded in fog. The mist is finer, suffusing the tops of the peaks in clouds and veiling the river from the sun, but not engulfing the scenery. The old dynasties respected this mist and the rains that came with it, for they knew that it helped crops grow and kept people alive. Some said that a goddess of fertility sent the rain for the benefit of the local population. So close became the connection between the rain and fertility that for the Chinese the phrase 'cloud and rain' came to stand for physical relations between a man and a woman.

In the middle of Wu Gorge is the small town of Peishi, which stands near the border between the provinces of Sichuan and Hubei. Its shops and stalls sell produce, such as apricots, Chinese chestnuts and persimmons, from the surrounding villages. Some of these settlements are disappearing as the water level rises as the Three Gorges Dam comes into full operation, but the river will flow on between the great peaks that surround Wu Gorge.

Wu Gorge twists and turns for some 45 km (28 miles). The dam has stilled the whirlpools, eddies and rapids that once kept riverboat captains on their toes. They told tales of quicksands

Above: Although Wu Gorge is being flooded, the upper slopes of its distinctive peaks will still rise above the waters. This is one aspect of the riverside scenery that the dam cannot alter.

Opposite: The builders of the traditional houses at Peishi used any material that was available locally: this house has a stone base, brick upper walls, and overhanging timber balconies.

and difficult currents, and needed just as much skill here as they did in Qutang. Here also, dangerous rocks were blasted away during the 1950s to make the passage safer.

TOWN ON THE MOVE

Wu Gorge comes to an end near the towns of Guandukou and Badong. Before the dam, regular travellers got used to passing Guandukou on the northern bank and Badong on the south. But to begin with, Badong was also on the river's northern bank, when it was part of the state of Ba. Under the Song dynasty the town was moved south, to bring it into Song territory. There it remained for centuries, developing into a busy modern town with factories, a power station, and quays where barges can dock to be loaded with goods. With the arrival of the Three Gorges Dam, however, Badong has moved once more. A new site has been selected back on the north bank, a few miles upstream. This is just one example of the huge effort needed to relocate entire populations whose homes and workplaces have been affected, or even wiped out, with the rising water level.

From Badong the river curves its way to Zigui, at the head of Xiling Gorge. Like many river towns hereabouts it had numerous old buildings, their mix of curved and stepped roofs making picturesque silhouettes. Some of these buildings have been rebuilt in new Zigui, where the residents have moved now the water has risen.

This area was the home of Qu Yuan (340–278 BC), one of China's best-loved poets. The Qu Yuan Memorial Hall, perched on the hillside above the river, is a local landmark with its white walls outlined in red and its curving parapets and upturned roofs. Inside are inscriptions and a statue of the poet dating from the Ming dynasty. Qu Yuan was attached to his homeland,

an area where oranges and tangerines grow in profusion; in fact, one of his most famous poems is an ode entitled 'In Praise of the Orange Tree'. In it, the poet hopes that he will have a long life and finally fade as the orange tree fades, 'and ever be your friend'.

Qu Yuan was an important official, chancellor to the king of Chu, but his rivals slandered him and he was forced from office. After a period of lonely wandering, the disconsolate poet threw himself into Dongting Lake, where he drowned. His wish to 'fade with the passing years' was unfulfilled. But he is remembered with affection here and all over the country with an annual dragon-boat festival and offerings of rice thrown into the river. His poems are universally quoted throughout China too.

XILING GORGE – ROCKS AND LEGENDS

The last of the Three Gorges, Xiling Gorge, is the longest at around 75 km (47 miles) and was historically the most dangerous to shipping, with a bewildering succession of rocks and rapids to try the patience and skill of even the most experienced river man. The worst of all was the area around a notorious rock known as 'Come to Me', where the navigable channel was both narrow and twisting. As riverboat captains concentrated on dodging rocks and negotiating the currents, everyone else on board looked on anxiously, never quite sure when the danger was past. Many of these obstacles were cleared during the 1950s, leaving both boatmen and passengers free to relax and enjoy the magnificent scenery.

The first section of Xiling Gorge has the picturesque name of Bingshu Baojian (Military Books and Precious Sword Gorge). This is a name that takes us straight away to the world of one of the Yangtze's great personalities, the military strategist Zhuge Liang (181–234). Zhuge was born at the end of the Han dynasty, when imperial power was breaking down and China split into three separate kingdoms – Wei in the north, Wu in the lower Yangtze region, and Shu in present-day Sichuan. Zhuge was military adviser to Liu Bei, king of Shu. Zhuge was a shrewd tactician. With his help, Liu Bei was able to defeat the armies of Wei, even though they were larger and stronger than his own. But Liu ignored his adviser's warnings and then went into battle against the mighty kingdom of Wu. Liu was defeated and lost his power, but Zhuge kept his reputation as an infallible strategist.

Above: Dragon boats are a popular spectacle on the Yangtze – and in Chinese communities everywhere. This example has a superbly painted dragon-head prow.

Overleaf: The scenery in Xiling Gorge is a mixture of cultivated terraces and steep cliffs, wooded slopes and bare peaks.

Legend says that Zhuge Liang travelled through Xiling Gorge towards the end of his life. He carried with him the books that he had written on military tactics. But after his king had refused to take his advice he was unsure that anyone would use his skills properly. So he hid his military books high on one of the cliffs above the gorge and also left his sword nearby. And there they became part of the landscape, in the form of a rock formation in layers, like a pile of books. A vertical rock nearby was said to be Zhuge's sword.

Not far away is a stretch of the river known as Micang Xia (Rice Granary Gorge). Here stands a high rock with a hole in it. The strong winds blow fine sand on to the rock, where it builds up and falls through the hole. The accumulating sand looks like a heap of rice, giving rise to the story that Zhuge Liang left a supply of food here for his soldiers.

These ancient legends give a hint of the rich store of metaphor inspired by Xiling's rock formations. Further up the gorge are two of the most bizarre examples. Niugan Mafei (Ox Liver and Horse Lungs Gorge). This extraordinary name comes from a pair of rock formations, one reddish-brown, another darker brown. But anyone expecting a lesson in animal anatomy on this stretch of the river should prepare to be disappointed. A British gunboat blasted a chunk out of the horse lungs in the time of Guangxu (1875–1908) and more damage was done by a Japanese ship during World War II. So all we can do now is simply marvel at the name.

The nearby Phoenix Rock is another name to marvel at, a rock that suggests the shape of a mythical bird next to another in the form of a warrior on horseback. Together they were known as 'Zhang Xiao Chases the Phoenix', an allusion to an old story about a young warrior who chased the magical bird, but could not reach it when it flew across the river.

Below: Zhuge Liang was the masterly strategist who was said to have hidden his military books above the river when his master ignored his advice.

Kongling Gorge, a stretch of the river with towering rocks and dramatic scenery, is only a short distance further downstream. The scene of more rapids, with greenish rocks glinting through the water, this reach was notorious, especially in the first half of the twentieth century when numerous steamboats were wrecked on the rocks. Now the waters are deeper by far. Beyond the gorge, mountains stretch for a great distance and are the home of exotic wildlife such as the golden cat whose upland habitat is threatened by the rising of the waters. For in this stretch of the Yangtze one becomes aware above all of the recent changes to the scene. Only a short distance of jagged rocks and soaring peaks remain before Sandouping, the site of the Three Gorges Dam itself.

THE THREE GORGES DAM

The first person to suggest building a dam across the Yangtze was Sun Yatsen, the political leader who became the father of the Chinese Republic. In 1919, Sun produced a paper called 'A Plan to Develop Industry', and in this was a proposal for controlling floods and improving irrigation by building a series of large dams. The greatest of all these dams was to be a barrier across the Yangtze, and Sun proposed that the obvious place to build such a barrier would be in the Three Gorges.

In spite of Sun's enthusiasm, there was neither the money nor the political stability needed in the 1920s to sustain such a huge project. The vast width and depth of the proposed structure, the millions of tonnes of material that would be required, the sheer volume of water that would be held back – all these things made the project simply too vast and too daunting in the 1920s. It remained a dream.

The idea was revived in the 1950s and 1960s, when it received the backing of Chairman Mao, who was keen for China to have the biggest hydroelectric dam in the world. Reacting to disastrous floods in the Yangtze area during the 1950s, Mao and his ministers were also convinced that the proposed dam could play a vital role in flood control. And there was another factor. If communist China could pull off this feat, they would achieve what generations of emperors had only dreamed of – they would tame the river that had terrorized the country with its floods and rapids for millennia. It would be, they supposed, a massive, world-beating triumph for the communist system.

But once again, the project came and went, stymied successively by economic depression in 1960 and by fears of sabotage in the late 1960s and early 1970s. By the 1980s, with advances

Above: The forest-dwelling golden cat is one of the rarer sights of the uplands above the gorges. The main threats to the species are hunting and the destruction of its forest habitat.

Left: Water pours through sluice gates as the river begins to back up behind the partly completed dam. This is one of many such changes made during the dam's construction, making local people increasingly aware of the enormous impact that this vast project will have on both the river and the land around it.

in engineering and strong political will backing the project, the dam seemed possible again. Feasibility studies began – but so too did mounting opposition to the idea of such a massive structure. As engineers argued over the exact site and politicians agonized about the budget, overseas construction companies encouraged the project in the hope of winning lucrative contracts. Meanwhile, many objectors, from engineers to archaeologists, went public.

These tensions, as with so many others, came to a head around the time of the disaster in Tiananmen Square, Beijing, in 1989, when the army moved in to halt a pro-democracy demonstration and many protesters were killed. Public debate about the dam was banned after the massacre, and in 1992 the plans were finally pushed through the National People's Congress, in spite of the fact that one third of the delegates either abstained or opposed the proposals. Given that the National Assembly invariably approved of government policy, such a level of objection was extraordinary. It was a signal that the controversy was far from over.

And given the sheer size of the project, this is hardly surprising. The facts and figures surrounding the Three Gorges Dam are staggering. The dam is 186 m (610 feet) high and will hold back a body of water around 175 m (575 feet) deep. The width of the structure will be 2092 m (6864 feet) – an unprecedented size for a concrete dam, although Egypt's Aswan High Dam, a rock-filled construction, is twice as wide. Around a quarter of a million workers have been employed on the project, many of them handling the nearly 26 million cubic metres (918 million cubic feet) of concrete required. This volume of raw material amounts to around twice that used for South America's Itaipu Dam, previously the world's largest concrete dam.

Above: Hundreds of workers, engineers and others – many of whom are long-standing employees of the dam project – watch as the reservoir begins to fill.

This massive barrier is designed to hold back the waters of an enormous reservoir, stretching more than 595 km (370 miles) through the gorges and beyond. More than 1300 villages and over 150 towns and cities have disappeared beneath these waters, forcing at least 1.25 million people to relocate to new homes. Thousands of sites of archaeological and architectural interest are affected – some have been moved, others have vanished for good. The dam's supporters believe that the project brings huge benefits that outweigh these drawbacks. It is time to look in more detail at the objections and to the responses of the government.

The simplest objection is to the sheer cost of the project. The dam's official price tag is 25 billion US dollars, and the government insists that the project is within budget. But critics claim that the finished dam may, in the end, cost as much as three times this amount, and that China can ill afford even the official bill.

For the dam's supporters, the justification comes with one of the project's main reasons for being: hydroelectric power. They claim that the dam will pay for itself when it starts to generate power, and the dam's capacity will be truly awesome. When work is finally completed, there will be twenty-six turbine generators, each capable of producing 700 megawatts of power. This is eight times as much electricity as that produced by Egypt's vast Aswan High Dam. To produce the same amount in a traditional coal-fired power station you would have to burn 40 million tons of coal. Supporters point to energy shortages in eastern and central China, and to the 60 million Chinese people who have no electricity supply at all. Bringing power to at least some of these people would improve their lifestyle and hasten the country's economic development. Not so, say the objectors. Since the economic reforms that took place in China in the late twentieth century, many state-owned enterprises have closed and electricity is being produced more efficiently, so there is now an excess of electricity available in many areas. And when cheaper sources of power come on stream, they will win out over electricity from the dam. Meanwhile, future demand for electricity is as difficult to predict as the country's economic development.

Another major issue is flood control. This was an additional reason for building the dam in the first place, and supporters say that the reservoir's massive storage capacity means that major downstream floods will be almost eliminated. Opponents, however, fear that the effect will not last. They predict that the river will deposit millions of tonnes of silt into the reservoir every year, and that in a short time its flood-control capacity will be reduced. What is more, they say, this extra sediment could actually make floods more likely near the upstream end of the vast reservoir, at Chongqing. Tried and tested measures, such as dykes and designated overflow areas, would have stood a better chance of controlling the floods, they claim, than turning the river into a deep, broad and increasingly silty lake with the Three Gorges Dam Project.

It is clear, though, that this wider, deeper river will be better for navigation. The rapids and eddies are disappearing, and when the project is complete the river will be able to take larger vessels much higher. The dam incorporates ship locks, and the increased traffic should cut transport costs and bring economic benefits to the upstream areas. But, again, the picture is not simple. Objectors predict that the increased silt will clog up some of the ports and Chongqing may suffer as a result.

Then there is the impact on the people who are forced to move. Officially, around 1.25 million people have been forced to relocate; the final figure may be many more. The Chinese government has assured them that they will be adequately compensated and re-housed, and the massive resettlement programme is already well under way. Some city families have moved to new accommodation built on higher ground near the river. Others, especially rural workers, are having to move to lands much further away. In practice, many people are ending up worse off. There are complaints that locals – especially those in rural areas – are not being consulted about their new homes and are often forced to move to areas with poorer land or fewer job opportunities. And as communities are dispersed, local cultures that have developed over centuries are wiped out. Supporters of the dam say that the objections are unfounded and that anyway the lives of the downstream peoples will improve vastly as a result of the new flood control.

But what about the environment? There is no argument that hydroelectricity is a comparatively 'clean' source of power – once the infrastructure is in place. But protesters are unhappy with the immense sacrifices that have to be made in order to achieve the dam's huge energy capacity. They fear that, with the river's natural power reduced, its waters will become more polluted as it can no longer flush factory waste out to sea. Then there is the question of habitat destruction. Many waterfowl, fish and other creatures live in and around the gorges. Their environment is being transformed and many will not be able to cope with the new regime of the river. Proponents of the dam claim that measures are being put in place to help these species. Many conservationists respond that the measures do not go far enough.

And then there is the sheer effect of the dam on the extraordinary scenery of the gorges. There is no doubt that the area will be transformed. The river will turn into a vast lake. Many of the landmark cliffs and rocks have already disappeared beneath the water. Yet the river is lined with mountains between 1005 m (3300 feet) and 1494 m (4900 feet) high and the water level will less than treble to 175m (575 feet) above sea level, so many rocks will remain unsubmerged and the water will still be bounded by dramatic cliffs and mountains. So, in spite of the fact that many people have rushed to see the gorges before the dam is finished, the rise in water level may not affect tourism as much as opponents fear.

Clearly, there is a debate to be had about all these alleged benefits and problems. But sadly, this debate is impossible in China itself because critics of the dam are suppressed. For example, engineer and investigative journalist Dai Qing is a powerful advocate both of press freedom and environmental protection. She has produced two books putting the case against the dam, which she has called 'the most environmentally and socially destructive project in the

world'. Dai Qing was imprisoned after the Tiananmen Square massacre. Her first book marshalling arguments against the dam, *Changjiang! Changjiang!* (*Yangtze! Yangtze!*) was banned in China. She has since been freed and allowed to travel, and has worked at both Harvard and Columbia universities. An inveterate campaigner, Dai Qing does not like being seen as a dissident. She actually tried to persuade the Tiananmen Square students to give up their protest. But her story indicates the powerful pressures the Chinese authorities have chosen to bring to bear on anyone who criticizes their policies.

Right: Signs on the sides of the gorges show the planned water level – 175 m (574 ft) is the projected depth of the new reservoir. Hundreds of thousands of people who lived below this marker have had to move.

Right: Even as the river rises, the daily life of the waterway continues. Barges like these take advantage of a deeper, broader channel between the peaks of Qutang's imposing mountains.

One of Dai Qing's principal criticisms of the dam is the possibility that it may burst, causing flooding and destruction on a disastrous scale. Just how disastrous can be illustrated by the story of the Banqiao Dam, which stretched across one of the Yangtze's tributaries in Henan province. The Banqiao, an earth and rock structure, was said to be very strong. But in August 1975, torrential storms raised the water to unprecedented levels. As it neared the top of the dam, engineers opened the sluice gates wide to let the excess through, but silting had caused a blockage and the water carried on rising. After three days of violent wind and rain, the water finally reached the top and the structure burst. In a matter of seconds a torrent engulfed the surrounding area, wiping out villages and killing perhaps as many as a quarter of a million people. China's government imposed a news blackout on the tragedy and information about it only found its way to the West in the 1990s.

Could a similar disaster happen in the Three Gorges? Engineers have raised serious questions about the geological stability of the area. The addition of a vast lake, its millions of tons of water pressing down on the nearby rocks, might cause earthquakes or land slips. There is a real fear that a land slip, for example, could produce massive waves, sending water over the lip of the dam or causing it to break up. As if this were not enough, cracks have been discovered in the dam's structure and attempts to repair them have met with mixed success. Again, the authorities stress the strength of the structure, but critics remain gravely concerned. Even premier Zhu Rongji seemed to be reflecting these concerns when he visited the dam in 1999. Remembering misgivings about the dam's strength, he warned those involved in the construction that it was up to them to build the dam to the highest standards: 'The responsibility on your shoulders is heavier than a mountain. Any carelessness or negligence will bring disaster to our future generations and cause irretrievable losses.'

The Three Gorges Dam is a vast structure and nothing quite like it has been built before. With a project of this size there are bound to be some problems, but it is hard to imagine that there will not be some benefits too. And the project is happening. The engineers are well into the final stage of the scheme. Stage One (1993–7) involved diverting the river and doing all the preparatory work. Stage Two (1997–2003) entailed building the dam itself and flooding the gorges behind it. Building the hydroelectric turbines and bringing the lake up to the full capacity are the main work of Stage Three (2003–9). And so the vast concrete barrier has emerged between the rocks of the Xiling Gorge. As it enters the final construction phase, the water level has risen. The protesters have no chance of stopping it now, although some of them still hope to persuade the authorities to reduce the planned height of the water. This 'second Great Wall' is becoming a fact of Chinese life.

Opposite: Old buildings like these, on the river's bank near Wuxi, have seen high water before, with waves threatening their walls. But this time the inundation is intended to be permanent.

CHAPTER 3

THE MIDDLE REACHES

In its middle course the Yangtze leaves behind the mountainous area of the Three Gorges and takes on a very different character between the cities of Yichang and Jiujiang. For the most part, it flows through the lowland country of Hubei province, and with the low-lying land come seasonal floods that have dominated the lives of the people and wildlife here for as long as anyone can remember.

Before the Three Gorges Dam and its smaller cousin the Gezhouba Dam were built, the river's waters poured out of the gorges and on to the flood plain. Once the heavy rains of summer began, flooding was inevitable and sometimes severe. With the coming of the great dam, the theory is that this will change. It will be possible to hold back much of the water and to control the flooding along the main course of the Yangtze, though not along its many tributaries.

Above: In the middle reaches, flooding has been part of life for thousands of years, and building barriers has become second nature. Here sandbags are being used to try to keep back the water.

But for now, the countryside of this part of Hubei province is still a landscape that has been shaped by floods. There are embankments along the river, and dykes, sluices and water-retention basins everywhere. All these are designed to contain powerful, swelling flood waters and all need regular maintenance and repair. As recently as the end of 2002, the Chinese government held a triumphant celebration to mark the completion of the latest reinforcement work on the dykes around Jiujiang, a response to the major flooding that took place in 1998. This is just the latest in a series of flood-protection measures that began in the Tang dynasty, when people first began to move into the area in large numbers and continued with great imperial projects during the Ming and Qing dynasties.

Below: Some stretches of the river bank are defended with earth ramparts, and traditional earth-moving methods, with picks, spades and panniers, are still used in many places.

Floods do not bring only an excess of water. Over the centuries, as the river and nearby lakes have overflowed into the countryside of Hubei and Jiangxi, they have deposited a rich silt. This can clog up the river bed, making regular dredging essential to keep the channels navigable. But it also brings layers of silt to the land, making the plain a fertile area, ideal for growing crops such as cotton and grain. So the region's agricultural success is bound to the river, which both fertilizes the soil and provides a route out of the area for exports. Those exports account for the majority of the traffic on the middle reaches of the river, much of it carried on groups of barges pulled along by tugs. There are smaller vessels, too, from local ferries to the little fishing sampans that provide an important portion of the region's diet. There are also cruise ships, for tourists who want to travel beyond the traditional sightseeing routes through the gorges, and take in towns such as Yichang.

YICHANG: BATTLE SITE AND TREATY PORT

An ancient town that has grown in recent years into a major city, Yichang lies at the downstream exit from the Three Gorges. Yichang has figured in Chinese history for more than 2000 years and is still remembered as the place where the forces of Shu and Wu fought a great battle during the Three Kingdoms period. In those days the town was known as Yiling.

The Shu leader Liu Bei commanded a huge army of some 700,000 men who gathered in the region. The Wu, by contrast, had only 50,000 troops under their general, Lu Xun. Lu knew well enough that his enemy had vastly superior forces, so he withdrew to the nearest local stronghold, Yiling. He saw that he could be surrounded here, but the mountainous terrain around the town made life difficult for the enemy. Stuck in the hills, the Shu could not mount a concerted attack and began to become demoralized. As time wore on, summer approached and the temperature rose. Conditions were sweltering in the uplands, so Liu Bei decided to come down to the cooler plains and set up camp. Here the Shu army regrouped and prepared to attack the Wu as soon as the temperature began to fall.

From his vantage point in Yiling, it was easy for Lu Xun's lookouts to see what was happening. Lu knew he would be defeated if he let the Shu come to him in the town, but he could not risk defeat in a pitched battle against vastly superior numbers in the lowlands. Then he remembered the strong east wind that blew across the plain in summer. Launching

a daring night attack, Lu and his men crept up on the enemy camp and set fire to some of their tents. The wind spread the flames quickly and soon the whole vast encampment of the Shu was ablaze. Most of the Shu were killed and Liu Bei gave up in despair. By biding his time, Lu Xun had triumphed over all the odds.

Yichang's position on the river has played a vital part in its history ever since. Until the end of the nineteenth century, large vessels were unable to navigate the Three Gorges, so Yichang was their last port of call before they had to turn round and begin their journey back downstream. So the town became an important port, where cargo was offloaded on to smaller craft so that goods could continue their journey up the Yangtze and along its tributaries, deeper into the country.

In the nineteenth century, the British seized on the town's key importance for trade and in April 1877 Yichang became one of the chain of treaty ports on the Yangtze. Treaty ports played a special role in nineteenth-century trade and in the expansion of Western influence in China. Such ports were set up by written agreement between the Western power and China. The port concerned then became open to foreign commerce, and a foreign-run customs office was set up in the town. There might also be Western courts and police officers, and Western boats would patrol the river.

In Yichang, British companies set up trading offices and built their own wharves on the river. The British controlled the customs office and levied duties. The place became a bustling centre of trade, where all sorts of boats, from large steamers and junks to smaller sampans, filled the river. By the time the larger vessels were regularly travelling up the gorges in the early 1890s, Yichang was well established as a port and retained its importance. It became a centre of the opium trade, levying taxes on the drug as it was brought from the provinces of Yunnan and Guizhou.

Parts of Yichang have been affected by the Three Gorges Dam, but the city has expanded higher above the river, and so hopes to continue to thrive in the twenty-first century. Some of its

Above: The river's width near Yichang gives room for vessels great and small. Many more are probably shrouded in the river mist.

historical sites will be preserved, notably the elegant Zixi Pavilion on the cliff above the Three Travellers' Cave, which commands a clear view of the entrance to Xiling Gorge. The cave itself commemorates the visits of two separate trios of travellers, one in the Tang dynasty and another in the Song.

The first travellers were three poets, the brothers Bai Zhuyi and Bai Xingjian and their companion Yuan Zhen. They inscribed poems on the walls of the cave before leaving. The second trio, a father and two sons of the Su family, passed here on their way to take the imperial civil service examinations in the capital. They also added poems, as have others who have since visited the cave. All were moved by the stunning mountain views, and some made the journey to nearby peaks, such as Camel Mountain, marvelling at the grandeur and stillness of the scenery.

GEZHOUBA: A PRECURSOR TO THE DAM

Like all the places affected by the Three Gorges Dam, Yichang will have its work cut out adapting to change. But the city is no stranger to the changes brought about by hydroelectric

Below: Statues of the Three Travellers of the Tang dynasty – the Bai brothers and their friend Yuan Zhen – can be seen near the cave where they stopped outside Yichang.

白行简　白居易　元　稹
Bai XingJian　Bai JuYi　Yuan Zhen

schemes because it has for some years been the site of the Gezhouba Dam, a kind of dress rehearsal for the Three Gorges project. As a result of this, Yichang has been coping with the presence of a vast engineering project and the advantages and perils of rapid industrial expansion for several decades, starting when the construction of the Gezhouba Dam began at the end of 1970.

By any standards other than those of the Three Gorges Dam, Gezhouba is huge. It is 2606 m (8550 feet) across, 54 m (177 feet) high, and holds back some 1.58 billion cubic metres (56 billion cubic feet) of water. Its generators are already producing over 15 billion kilowatts of electricity per year, and this will increase when the larger dam comes into operation. Gezhouba is also designed to act in concert with the Three Gorges Dam, regulating the flow of tail water from the larger dam. It is a dramatic structure, not least the vast locks in which ships travel from one level to another. Cargo ships of 10,000 tonnes can pass through these locks, and the huge carrying capacity of such vessels has stimulated local industry. Once known as a centre for traditional products such as terracotta, Yichang is now home to hundreds of factories producing everything from electronic goods to textiles, machines to paper.

THE CHINESE STURGEON: A LIVING FOSSIL

Above: Gezhouba has enormous locks so that large ships can sail up and down the river past the dam's walls. The lock gates, with their latticework of steel struts, braced to resist the massive pressure of the water behind, are feats of engineering in themselves.

Yichang has become a special place for one of the most amazing creatures of the Yangtze River. On the islet of Shuixita is the Chinese Sturgeon Institution, an organization that is devoted to the study of the river's largest creature. The Chinese sturgeon has swum in the area for some 140 million years and is one of those creatures that has justly earned the description of 'living fossil'. It is an awesome fish that, when fully grown, can reach a length of 4 m (13 feet), making it the biggest of all sturgeons.

Although it is known mainly in the Yangtze's tributaries, for millions of years the Chinese sturgeon took the whole river as its habitat, from the coast to above Chongqing. In late summer and early autumn every year, shoals of Chinese sturgeon swam from the coastal regions to their spawning grounds above the Three Gorges. The fish would stop in places where the current was strong and the river bed was steep and pebbly, and here they would lay their eggs. After hatching, the young together with their parents swam back down to the Eastern and Yellow seas, where the young fish grow towards maturity.

The damming of the river has disrupted this breeding cycle and prevented the fish making their upriver journey. Other factors, such as fishing, have also put the species under threat. So the scientists of the Chinese Sturgeon Institution are using artificial breeding methods to help this endangered species to survive. It is hoped that this work will be complemented by the new Chinese sturgeon nature reserve recently established on the east coast of Congming Island, Shanghai, at the seaward end of the fish's range. It is hoped that the conservation effort will eventually lead to a revival in the fortunes of this imposing creature.

Above: It is hoped that the fortunes of the Chinese sturgeon, a rare sight today in the waters of the Yangtze, will be helped by the conservation measures put in place by scientists in Yichang and Shanghai.

JINGZHOU AND SHASHI: TWIN CITIES

Downriver from Yichang the true lowlands begin as the river leaves behind the mountains and cliffs and begins to cross the Jianghan Plain. This is a rich, low-lying area, famous for growing cotton as well as for a range of food products, such as beans and grain. The river is broader and slower here, flowing in great curving meanders that curl their way across the plain. Around 48 km (30 miles) from Yichang – and much less as the crow flies – the river comes to the twin cities of Jingzhou and Shashi.

Jingzhou was once the greater of the pair. Under its old name of Jiangling, it was a regional capital as early as 2000 BC, was chief city of the Kingdom of Chu during the Spring and Autumn period, and was also a prominent city in the Three Kingdoms period. It was in the latter, when, according to legend, the town walls were built by the hero Guan Yu (*c.* AD 160–219). Guan Yu was a notable warrior known both for his superhuman strength and his unmatched loyalty. Long after his death he was deified, and devotees of Chinese popular religion still know him as the god of war. It is a mark of Jiangling's importance that its walls were said to have been built by such a powerful figure.

Nowadays the old city is overshadowed by its modern twin, Shashi, originally the river port for Jiangling and now a manufacturing centre. The place came to prominence during the 1850s, as the result of a disaster downstream. During the Taiping Rebellion of the mid-nineteenth century, the rebels captured Nanjing in 1853 and paralysed trade downstream of Shashi. This meant that boats coming eastwards from the interior of China had little alternative but to stop at Shashi and unload, so the port became a key distribution centre for a wide area.

In a short time Shashi had developed a superb series of trade links and became a rich prize. In 1895 it was opened up to foreign business, and a number of overseas merchants made their fortunes in the town. Notable among these were the Japanese, who traded in the seeds of the cotton plants that grew on the Jianghan Plain.

The city was also strongly religious, and Buddhism had its adherents both among the local Chinese and the Japanese traders. Some of their temples and pagodas survive, and one of the landmarks of the Shashi region is the Wanshoubao Pagoda, a seven-storey riverside structure. It was once part of a larger temple complex and still displays carved reliefs of the Buddha. Pagodas were built all along the Yangtze during the Tang dynasty, when Buddhism reached its first peak of popularity in China. This example is later, from the Ming dynasty, but it is good that it still overlooks the river when so many Buddhist monuments have disappeared.

DONGTING LAKE: FLOOD AND FERTILITY

The river continues its meandering journey across the plain from Shashi. Flowing in a general southeasterly direction, it is linked hereabouts by several of its tributaries to Dongting Hu, China's second largest lake. Dongting Lake is one of China's great sights – a beautiful, seemingly endless sheet of water, dotted with sampans, its gently moving surface reflecting the sun. It has inspired poets and writers who have visited it, such as the Lao dynasty poet Fan Zhongyan, who wrote:

> *The distant hills caressing,*
> *It takes the river's flooding.*
> *Its waves are ever rolling*
> *From morning light to evening*
> *The view is ever changing.*

The poet soaked up the peace as, like thousands before and after, he drank in the views and relished the refreshing breeze.

Yet Dongting Lake has not always been peaceful. In earlier dynasties the imperial navy used its vast expanse of water on which to practise manoeuvres, and a tall watchtower was put up so that commanders could check on their ships' progress. The tower's successor is still there, dating only from 1985, but built in the style of the Song dynasty, with striking yellow tiles. Next to the tower is the so-called Thrice Drunken Pavilion. This building commemorates the god Lu

THE MIDDLE REACHES

Dongbin, who is said to have got drunk here three times, but on one of these occasions managed to keep his wits about him enough to save the tower from falling down.

Today, there are no more naval manoeuvres, but the waters themselves have to be watched. The fringes of the lake are lined with earth banks to hold back the flood water, and often these

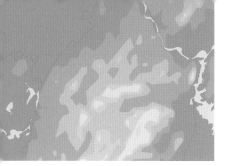

barriers get close to breaking. The lake has been compared to a vast balloon that gradually fills up until it is ready to explode. When it fills like this it is time for the locals to mount a constant vigil. Every 100 m (330 feet) or so, someone is posted to keep guard on a stretch of bank. Any hint of a crack or a weakness has to be mended immediately. If the watcher ignores such a break, the land could be inundated and the crops destroyed.

Thousands of people live around the banks of the lake. In a country with a population the size of China, good farmland is in short supply, and the silt-rich land around Dongting Lake is very fertile. But this silty fertility is a problem as well as a benefit. For years the farmland has been encroaching on the lake. Thousands of hectares have been reclaimed for farming, and the area is criss-crossed with more than 6,000 ditches for irrigation and drainage, controlled by countless sluices. As a result of this land reclamation, Dongting Lake is now around half the size it was fifty years ago. That is 50 per cent less capacity for storing flood water, or twice as much danger for the farmers and their families. Hence the endless vigilance and the hard work with sandbags. It is a powerful example of the precarious existence that many people in the Yangtze region have to endure.

Below: An artist's evocative impression of Red Cliff conveys the precipitous outline of the rock and the river mist that subsumes everything in the middle distance.

RED CLIFF: A HERO TRIUMPHS

Near Dongting Lake is the site of a famous battle, the Battle of Red Cliff, fought in the year 208 during the Eastern Han dynasty when China was breaking up into the Three Kingdoms. At this time the kingdoms of Shu and Wu allied themselves with the powerful kingdom of Wei. The Wei already dominated northern China, and wanted to take over the area around the Yangtze, then ruled by Liu Bei, king of Shu.

Liu Bei was familiar with the might of the Wei and saw that he would not be able to face them alone, so he called upon the king of Wu to help him. But even their combined forces were not enough to withstand an attack from Wei, which at this time had an army of around 200,000 men. But Liu Bei had one great advantage, his wily military adviser Zhuge Liang.

Zhuge knew that Wei's vast army would be useless without a decent supply of arms. The forces of Wei were rather well supplied, but Zhuge was short of arrows so he devised a scheme to acquire a stock of them from

THE MIDDLE REACHES

Above: The russet colours
of both earth and rocks in
this area show how Red
Cliff got its name.

the very force arrayed against him. Waiting until the fog came down on the river one night, he had a fleet of naval junks loaded with straw bales covered in black cloths. Then he sent the junks along the river, their crews concealed but beating drums loudly in a tattoo to suggest that they were making an attack. As Zhuge hoped, the Wei armies gathered and launched an all-out assault on the boats, firing arrows at the black-shrouded bales until they looked like pincushions. But the junks simply sailed serenely on until they were out of range. The Wei had lost thousands of arrows, which wily Zhuge then issued to his own soldiers.

Then Zhuge played another trick on the Wei. He told one of his spies to infiltrate the Wei camp and get a message to their leader. The message was that there would soon be an attack and that the Wei should moor all their boats together. That way, it was suggested, the Wei soldiers, who had had many victories on land but were unused to fighting on water, would have a safe, steady firing platform. But with all the boats tethered together – and most of Wei's troops on board – it was easy for the forces of Shu and Wu to defeat them. As at Yichang, fire was the fatal weapon. The men of Shu and Wu started a blaze that raged quickly across the boats. The scorching heat of the flames, it was said, turned the rocks of the cliff red, the colour they have been ever since. The red rocks and the thousands of weapons from the Three Kingdoms period found nearby and displayed on the site are vivid reminders of this famous victory and of the cunning of Zhuge Liang, who is one of the heroes of the Yangtze River – and of China as a whole.

WUHAN: TEA AND OPIUM

As the river continues its wandering course across the plain of Jianghan, it crosses an area that is more and more dominated by water. Dongting is the largest lake, but there are countless others, many of which surround the important cities of Wuhan and Jiujiang. Added to the many tributaries that join the river in this region, the thousands of drainage channels, and the raised river banks designed to protect the towns from floods, and one can see that the whole area is a liquid landscape.

From a distance, Wuhan looks like a big modern city, its skyscrapers and shops glistening with the high-tech sheen of twenty-first-century China. But it is actually three cities in one – Hankou, Wuchang and Hanyang – and each of these places, which have grown and gradually merged together, has its own identity and history.

Hankou is the commercial centre, a city that grew from a small fishing port to become a major international centre in the nineteenth century. It is the best known of the three cities to outsiders because it became a Treaty Port in 1861 and has been a centre for trade ever since. Five foreign powers set up concessions here – Britain, France, Germany, Japan and Russia. Their headquarters were along the north bank of the river, and some of their buildings survive along the embankment. They were at their busiest in the fifty years after the Treaty Port was set up, which was the period when opium was being imported to China and ships packed with the drug sailed up the Yangtze as far as Hankou. The quays were always busy with ships from as

Below: For all its history, Wuhan is a modern city, full of tall office towers and other commercial buildings that serve a busy traffic on the river.

far afield as London and New York, and foreign merchants grew rich from the trade. And they had a good life. The city boasted one of the best-appointed clubs in China, there was a golf course, and one of Hankou's two racecourses was set aside for the use of foreigners so that the people of the Treaty Port could enjoy the sport of kings.

It was not just opium that was bought and sold here. The traders of Hankou were importing useful materials, such as iron and cement, and bringing in a vast range of manufactured goods that were not available locally – everything from pins to matches. Their exports were local goods that ranged from the luxurious (such as silk, animal skins and musk) to the typical everyday products of China – for example, rice, bean cake, sesame oil and bran. Above all,

Above: At night fountains, fireboats and floodlights dazzle the viewer on Jiujiang's vibrant waterfront. As well as demonstrating the influence of Western consumerism, the sight reminds one of a more traditional Chinese spectacle – the firework display.

there was tea. Packed into wooden tea chests (another import), the black, green, brick, oolong and other varieties of tea brought prosperity to the traders of Wuhan.

As a headquarters of the tea trade, Wuhan was also the starting point of the annual China Tea Races. The races began because two special factors came together – a valuable commodity that fetched high prices in Europe and a means of transporting that commodity at high speed. The commodity was tea, loved in Britain and grown in China. The fast transport was provided by the clippers – light, sleek ships that carried a vast square-footage of sail and could travel faster than anything else on the oceans.

The race was to get the tea of the new harvest to Europe as quickly as possible. The tea arrived in Hankou in May each year, and the fleets of the British, Russian and American merchants were there waiting for it. So were the various countries' tea buyers (or *chazi*), whose job it was to taste the tea and do the deal without delay. Once this was done, the clippers were loaded and the great race began – downriver to the Red Buoy that marked the mouth of the Yangtze, south to Singapore, and then off to London. The total 25,748-km (16,000-mile) voyage could take as little as 97 days, and even over this great distance, the leading ships could arrive in port with less than 24 hours between them. For the winner there was tremendous kudos, and the best price from British buyers, who were eager to get their hands on the first tea of the new harvest.

The races went on through the late nineteenth century, surviving even the rise of the steamships and the consequent demise of the elegant clippers. But the tradition went into decline after the late 1880s, when more and more tea began to be exported from India. Even then, though, the port had enough traffic from other trade to keep it thriving. Junks filled the harbour and their crews rushed ashore to taste the delights of the city. They could buy many of their supplies from floating shops, brightly coloured boats with symbols of their wares hung from their masts. But most were soon tempted on to the river bank to explore the town. Here, in a maze of narrow streets, bustling to the gutters with every class from coolie to merchant and ringing with a

Opposite: For all its modernity, Hankou is still a place where many people hang out their washing above the street, buy their vegetables from a barrow, and travel around on foot.

Below: Old Wuhan, a tightly knit community of white-rendered shops and houses, was a centre for the junks and clippers of the lucrative tea trade.

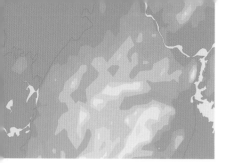

babble of languages from Mandarin to Russian, a dark world of entertainment opened up to them. They could sample Hankou's interesting riverine cuisine and, above all, they could visit its notorious opium dens (see page 148).

But the prosperity and the good life were not to last. In 1911 came revolution, and Hankou was caught up in the heat of battle. Revolutionaries and the imperial army fought on the city streets, and many buildings were destroyed in the ensuing fires. The area took another assault in 1938 during the Sino-Japanese War and became a hotbed of political activity during the late 1940s.

From the earliest days of the Treaty Port to the 1940s, there was always much to do in Hankou, and, although the darkest dives have long since gone, some of the old port's atmosphere is still preserved around the Customs House on the embankment and in the area around the railway station. In this district there are narrow streets and alleys packed with markets and jammed with walkers dodging pedicabs. There is plenty of fare for the adventurous – local delicacies still range from river fish to frogs and snails.

The place is thriving economically, with bustling shops and markets that attract visitors drawing up in cruise ships in increasing numbers from both Shanghai and Chongqing. But it is all at a price. Many of the traditional European-style buildings, put up in the times of the Treaty Port, are being knocked down. The old narrow alleys are disappearing. Glass and steel nightclubs, hotels and shopping malls are springing up in their place. The urban scene becomes more and more like something from the West, in a twenty-first-century version of the development that took place in the late nineteenth century.

Hanyang shares the north bank with Hankou, but is separated from it by the Han River, a tributary of the Yangtze. The expansion of this part of the city dates from the time of the Qing emperors, when an arsenal and manufacturing centre was established here. The place is still known for steel factories and other heavy industry, but also boasts the delightful Guqin Tai (Lute Platform), a series of gardens and courtyards built in memory of two musicians who lived, it is said, around 2000 years ago. When on a visit to Hanyang, one of the pair, Yu Baiya, played his lute, but only the other lutenist, Zhong Ziqi, really appreciated the artistry of the performance. As a result, the two became friends. They had to part company, but agreed to meet the following year in Hanyang. But when Yu returned he found that Zhong had died. Distraught, he played a farewell piece in memory of his friend, then tore the strings off his instrument and vowed never to play again. Today the Lute Platform is a haven within the gardens of the Workers' Cultural Palace, and is also the scene of Chinese opera productions.

The third of Wuhan's trio of cities, Wuchang, occupies the south bank. It is the oldest of the three, and was a regional capital during the Yuan dynasty. It is famous for its vast lakes, gardens and museums, and is also the site of Huang He Lou (Yellow Crane Tower), a fine building with yellow tiles that has been praised by many Chinese poets. The name of the tower derives from a legend about a Taoist sage who was carried off to immortality on the back of a crane. Ever since, cranes have been symbols of long life, and the tower, with its beautiful views over city and river, has been famous. Like many 'ancient' buildings in China, it has been rebuilt many times. The current incarnation dates from the 1980s, but is still beautiful.

Immediately to the west of Hankou is a famous red cliff on the northern bank of the river. This cliff has a special place in the life of one of China's greatest writers, the poet Su Dongpo (1037–1101), who lived during the Song dynasty. Su was a high official in the Northern Song capital, but was sacked when he dared to oppose some new laws. He was exiled to Hankou and given the lowly post of assistant commissioner to the local militia. He liked to sail his boat along the stretch of river below the red cliff, and it became a favourite spot for Su Dongpo and his friends. One of his poems describes the military victory that took place at the other red cliff, near Dongting, and he must have compared the two places when he arrived in Hankou. Another poem bemoans his exile as he nears the end of his life far from the northern capital where he began his career:

> When the night falls on the veranda,
> Leaves are already rustling in the wind….
> Who will enjoy with me
> This lonely night of mid-autumn?
> Holding my cup up to heaven,
> I look with sadness to the north.

Today pavilions dedicated to the poet crown the cliff, and lovers of Song dynasty poetry make the pilgrimage to them.

THE CHAIRMAN AND THE RIVER

It was at Wuhan that Mao Zedong returned to the Yangtze in 1956, some 21 years after he had crossed the river on his epic Long March. Back in 1935, crossing the river with his long column of followers had been both a challenge and a symbol, as Mao and his men commandeered a fleet of boats from the locals, ferried their way over and set up their new base in the province of

Left: Mao Zedong's house is a few minutes from the river near Wuhan, protected from floods by a tree-lined bank. It is close to several places that have strong links to the chairman, including the spot where he swam the river and the Peasant Movement Institute, which he directed in 1926 and 1927.

Sichuan. (For more detail about the Long March see Chapter 1.) For the marching communists, far from certain of their future, this successful crossing of the Yangtze was like a victory over one of the forces of nature.

The Yangtze, together with China's other great rivers, the Pearl and Xiang, kept their potent symbolism for the communist leader. For Mao, these rivers ran like great veins and arteries through China, bringing life and livelihood to those who lived and worked on their banks. But with their strong currents and overwhelming floods, they could also bring danger and death. Mao saw their elemental force as a power to be mastered and, proud of his fitness and athletic ability, felt he could master the Yangtze by swimming across. By doing so, Mao faced diverse risks – the river's fabled and treacherous currents, poisonous snakes, parasite-carrying worms that could give him bilharzia. But that was the point – the greater the hazard, the greater the triumph.

And there were other reasons for such a public gesture of strength. In 1956, things were not going well for China's leader. Party grandees were fighting and arguing with each other. Opposition to Mao's reforms was building up in many places – in Wuhan especially. Seven years after the foundation of the People's Republic, the people's enthusiasm for his leadership seemed to be on the decline. Mao's risky and dramatic gesture was designed to make people notice and respect his prowess, and rekindle their enthusiasm for Mao as leader and man of revolutionary action.

The swim, and his other similar swims in later years, did just that. Mao's popularity escalated, and, for good or ill, his policies found widespread support. The chairman recorded his swim in a famous poem, which was to be much quoted by his followers:

> *Now I am swimming across the great Yangtze*
> *Looking up to the open sky of Chu.*
> *Let the wind blow and the waves beat –*
> *Better far than an aimless stroll in a courtyard.*
> *Today I am at ease:*
> *It was by a stream that the master said –*
> *'Life – like the waters – rushes into the past!'*

The lines sum up Mao's defiance of the river, his high moral stance, and his insistence that the past is flowing away. And even today, his followers, not content with merely quoting his words, organize swims of the Yangtze every year to commemorate his daring feat.

Mao's poem continues with a glance towards the future. He describes how great building projects will also conquer the Yangtze, first of all the new bridge that was being built to link Hanyang and Wuchang and that opened in 1957, then the great barrier of the Three Gorges Dam. Mao foretold how the dam would hold back the clouds and rain 'till a smooth lake rises in the narrow gorges'. Swimming the Yangtze and building the dam were two of Mao's pet projects, one conquering the river on a small scale, one on a scale unparalleled in human history.

Above: Photographs like this, showing Mao Zedong swimming the Yangtze, were reproduced all over China to show the chairman's bravery in tackling this demanding and dangerous feat.

JIUJIANG: CITY OF NINE RIVERS

Downstream from Wuhan the river runs roughly southwest through a valley between the Dabie and Mufu Mountains. Running generally parallel to the river a short distance away is the railway, which was eventually to take much of the traffic away from the water. Both converge on

Below: Not far from Poyang Lake, a farmer waits for ducks to cross in front of his cattle.

Right: The setting sun creates an image of tranquility above the rich, silty waters of Poyang Lake.

Jiujiang; in fact, much more converges on this town, since its name means 'nine rivers', a reference to the watercourses that flow into the vast lake, Poyang Hu, greater even than Dongting in both size and importance. The lakes, rivers and mountains bring this large city its first claim to fame – it is set in an area of great natural beauty. Jiujiang is also famous for its literary connections and its importance in the history of Buddhism.

For centuries, visitors have been impressed by the beauty of the city's setting. The original town lines the river and surrounds two small lakes, Gantang and Nanhu, nearby. In the distance the view is set off by mountains, which virtually surround the city. Between the peaks are low-lying areas containing larger lakes. Above everything towers the tallest and most beautiful of the nearby peaks, Lushan, with pine trees clinging to its cliffs and wisps of cloud clinging to the pine trees.

One of the people who admired the views here was a Tang dynasty poet, Bai Juyi, who worked as an official in Jiujiang. He liked watching the reflections in the water and one of his poems includes the line, 'I saw the moon drenched by the river'. He decided to build himself a house on a tiny island in Gantang Lake, and this building became known as the Drenched Moon

Left: Neng Rem Pagoda in Jiujiang rises high above the city. Its carved stone structure is a rare survival here from the Song dynasty.

Pavilion. Later the pavilion was rebuilt during the Song and Qing dynasties, and was renamed the Yanshui (Misty Water) Pavilion, the name it still bears today. Several other old buildings survive in the town, including two notable pagodas. One, the Suo Jiang Ta, a six-sided, seven-storey pagoda, built in 1585, that stands close to the river embankment. The other, at Neng Ren Temple, also has seven storeys and is even older, dating to the Song dynasty.

Monks and philosophers were just as captivated by the scenery as poets. A notable monk who came here was Hui Yuan (334–416), who settled in a wooded area at the foot of Lushan. In those days this was a lonely place, where a monk could find peace, the quiet broken only by the cries of gulls from the river or cranes from the lakes. Here among the peaks and pine trees Hui Yuan developed a new form of Buddhism, imagining that those who followed Amitabha, the Buddha of Compassion, would be reborn in a wonderful 'Pure Land' or paradise in the west. Known as Pure Land Buddhism, the new religion began to attract followers, and 123 people, among them monks from India and Nepal, soon joined Hui Yuan. They built Dong Lin Temple for him and it became famous as monks spread the ideas of Pure Land Buddhism across China. By the Tang dynasty, Dong Lin Temple was a thriving place of scholarship, with a large library and a centre for translating Buddhist scriptures. Today, the temple still survives, although the community of monks is much smaller.

The fame of Hui Yuan brought many visitors to Lushan, and, like modern tourists, they marvelled at the year-round natural beauty. In spring they enjoyed the beauty of the peach blossoms and azaleas that covered the local hills. In summer they found that the temperature on the slopes offered a welcome break from the often oppressive heat and humidity of Jiujiang. In autumn, the changing colours of the leaves on the trees provided a new source of pleasure and beauty. In winter there were still the marvellous rock formations, the overhanging cliffs and the caves. By the late nineteenth century, Jiujiang was a thriving Treaty Port and many of the visitors to Lushan were foreign merchants. Some fell in love with the place and built holiday homes in the area, establishing the small town of Guling, a settlement of merchants' and missionaries' summer bungalows, which still largely survives.

POYANG: HOME OF THE SIBERIAN CRANE

The residents of Guling lived well above the river, and in the nineteenth century preferred to be carried up the hill in sedan chairs. From the mountain they could look down not only on China's greatest river, but also on Poyang, the country's largest lake. As they watched, they would have

seen one of the transport hubs of this part of China, alive with junks and sampans carrying locally produced grain, tea, bamboo and fine porcelain from the factories at nearby Jingdezhen. They knew that the lake's waters were also full of fish, including delicacies such as anchovies and whitebait and that the place was also highly attractive to the local bird population.

Today Poyang, like its sister lake Dongting, is smaller than it used to be due to land reclamation. But it is also now protected. A vast nature reserve stretches along the western side of the lake, where the authorities ensure that there is a good home for the tens of thousands of birds – especially cranes, swan geese and ducks – that arrive to spend the winter here. It is an awesome sight, as the mudflats expand during the winter, to see thousands of these birds arriving. Sometimes the flock of swan geese, for example, has been estimated at around 50,000, while the total bird population of the lake may in some years be as high as half a million. The Dalmatian pelican, black-faced spoonbill, oriental stork, and great bustard are some of the more spectacular species that may be seen here in winter, but many others flock to wade and feed in the rich mud of the lake's margins.

Poyang is also the winter home of one of the area's endangered birds, the Siberian crane, and up to 3000 of these birds make the journey from eastern Siberia every year. The Siberian crane is a highly specialized bird that can live only in wetlands. The cranes from eastern Siberia depend entirely on Poyang Lake for their winter quarters and they need the annual rhythm of flood and mud to continue. After the summer floods, the waters of the lake shrink dramatically in winter, leaving acre upon acre of mudflats, wet grasslands and shallow water – the perfect habitat for waders like the crane. There is a widespread fear that, with the Three Gorges Dam in operation, the flooding of Poyang will be controlled, affecting the cranes' wintering area and putting this rare species in further danger. This is one of the environmental questions that hangs over the dam project, suggesting how the vast barrier may affect the life and habitat of creatures who have for centuries lived far downriver from the dam site itself.

A good vantage point to look down on both the lake and the Yangtze is Shizhong Shan (Stone Bell Hill) near Hukou and the mouth of Poyang. The hill gets its name from its bell-like shape and from the odd ringing sounds made by the water splashing against the rocks at its foot. It was once a military stronghold. During the Taiping Rebellion in 1853, rebel commander Shi Dakai

Opposite: Shizhong Shan, a popular viewpoint, is also the site of several buildings dating back to the Qing dynasty.

Above: A Siberian crane makes itself at home among the damp grasslands near Poyang Lake. The bird's winter food is made up of the tubers of the plants that grow along the margins of the lake.

Right: The 'miniature mountain' of Xiaogu Shan, dominated by the pale walls of Qisu Temple, is one of the most surprising sights on the Yangtze.

built a fortress here and guarded the entrance to the lake against the imperial forces. The Qing general, Zeng Guofan, attacked the rebels with a fleet of war junks, but was badly defeated. He put up a memorial plaque to those who lost their lives, and this survives near the remains of the rebels' stronghold. Now the hill is a peaceful viewpoint, and visitors come, just as poets like Su Dongpo did in the Song dynasty, to admire the river scenery and marvel at the magical sound of the water ebbing and flowing below.

XIAOGU SHAN: A MINIATURE MOUNTAIN

A few miles to the east is one of the river's most extraordinary sights, one that could be said to mark the downstream end of the middle reaches. This is Xiaogu Shan, a rocky outcrop that looks like a tiny mountain, joined by mudflats to the Yangtze's northern bank. Bamboo clings to the sides of its steep peak and a couple of buildings, with white walls and grey roofs, cling to the slopes, looking as if they could slide off and disappear into the water in a puff of wind.

These buildings belong to the Qisu Temple, which has been here since the Song dynasty and is still home to a small number of monks. It is a tough climb up to the temple, or to the peak beyond, and the pilgrim or visitor must hold tightly on to chains that are provided for the purpose. Many of the pilgrims who come here are childless women, who make offerings to the temple's goddess, Xiaogu Niang Niang, in the hope that they will bear children.

At the very top of this miniature mountain is a tablet that tells Xiaogu's story. Xiaogu was a girl from Fujian who was betrothed to a local boy called Peng Liang. But her parents died when she was still young, and she was adopted by a local Taoist sage and lost touch with her betrothed. Xiaogu became a learned Taoist, and vowed to devote herself to a chaste life of scholarship, but one day when out gathering herbs she fell, injured herself and was rescued by a woodcutter – who turned out to be Peng Liang. The two renewed their betrothal and seemed destined for happiness, but the sage, resentful that she had broken her vow, had her imprisoned. A friendly monk helped her escape, and the couple fled up the river, but the sage pursued them and eventually turned them into two hills, Pengliang Ji on one side of the river, Xiaogu Shan on the other. This charming story of Xiaogu Shan is typical of the way in which landscape, history and myth come together along the middle reaches of the Yangtze.

CHAPTER 4

THE LOWER REACHES

Below Anqing, the Yangtze winds its last few hundred kilometres towards the coast and the East China Sea. In this area it flows mostly through a lowland region built up from layers of river silt. These are some of the most fertile parts of China, and the traveller is never far from water. Everywhere you look there are rice fields, the extent of which are so vast that it is no surprise that the river basin produces about 70 per cent of China's paddy rice. But the region is productive in other ways, too. It has accounted for nearly half of China's fish catch, though this figure is changing now that the government has enforced fishing restrictions to conserve stocks. The area also contains some of the country's greatest cities, such as Nanjing and Shanghai, which are major industrial and financial centres. For food production and commerce, this is the beating heart of China.

Above: Anqing, on the northern bank of the river, is one of the Yangtze's leafier cities.

This triangular-shaped region is often referred to as the Yangtze delta, but it is not a delta like that of the Nile, which has a multitude of channels flowing towards the sea and no main estuary. In the distant past, it is true, the Yangtze did have several separate channels, but most of these have long silted up. However it still has a true estuary, awesomely wide, near Shanghai. This river mouth, several kilometres wide, is clearly visible on maps. The delta area is, however, criss-crossed with water courses and unified by its low-lying country and fertile soil. And the area is distinctive in various ways – it is the region of cotton growing and fishing, and it is where, since the nineteenth century at least, Chinese and overseas cultures have mixed in a unique and potent way.

Above all, these cultures have come together in trade. For hundreds of years, river junks – and latterly modern craft – have been hauling vast quantities of goods up and down the river, and out to sea. Basic commodities such as rice and salt, luxury goods such as silk and tea (for before the twentieth century tea was expensive and China produced the best) – are products that have brought traffic and wealth to the Yangtze. And a world of infrastructure and support networks grew up around this trade. Shipbuilding and docking, banking, even entertainment for those working on the river: all these businesses have influenced the settlements that have grown up along the Yangtze, and no more so than on the busy lower reaches.

Above: These workers are planting rice, one of the principal crops of the region, and a key reason why China depends so heavily on the fertility of the lower Yangtze area.

In Ming and Qing times, Chinese trade was highly organized, with merchants of each trade forming bodies called *hui-kuan*, a term meaning literally 'assembly halls', but which refers both to the trade guilds and the buildings in which they met. The guilds provided gathering places for traders, supervision over businesses and prices, and a way of putting pressure on government officials to the benefit of trade and industry. The guilds also organized social and religious events, from festivals celebrating the gods who presided over specific trades or businesses to elaborate parties. And they exercised lifelong care of their members, even helping needy families with funeral expenses. There were guilds all over China, but they were especially strong in the Yangtze valley, where trade played such a vital part in life.

In some cases, trade sprang up purely because the river was an ideal form of transport. But in others, it was the products of the lower Yangtze itself that were being bought and sold. Rice is an obvious example. Silk is another, for the lower reaches of the Long River were one of the major centres of silk production, an industry that the Chinese guarded jealously for centuries, keeping its processes secret and its prices high. This skilled and laborious industry was well suited to the region. Mulberry, the silk moth's food and habitat, grows well here. And the area's network of rivers and canals is ideal for the transport required at each stage in production: cocoons need to be taken to reeling mills, yarn to different locations for dyeing and weaving, and so on to the finished cloth, which was carried along the Yangtze and its tributaries to markets in China and overseas. Westerners think of the long overland route – the Silk Road – as the main pathway for silk travelling from China to the West. But the Yangtze played its part too, its ships travelling out into the East China Sea towards the Indian Ocean and far beyond.

ANQING TO WUHU

The first city on the lower reaches is Anqing, set in the hills on the river's northern bank. It is an old city, a local capital under the Qing and during the republican period, but has few old buildings because these were largely destroyed during the Taiping Rebellion (see page 135). Its one famous old landmark is the seven-storey Zhenfeng Pagoda, built in 1570 and designed by Zhang Wencai, an architect who came from Beijing. Within are some 600 images of the Buddha; outside, the pagoda boasts six octagonal balconies built in stone and partly hiding the structure's brick walls.

Below: Thin fibres unravel from the cocoons of the silk moth in a local industry that still relies heavily on traditional skill and handwork.

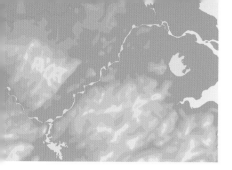

To the south of Anqing are the peaks of Juihuashan (Nine Brilliant Mountains), one of the most sacred sites for Chinese Buddhists. It is a place of great natural beauty up to 1341 m (4400 feet) above sea level, where many come to soak up the atmosphere of spiritual calm. The nine-peaked mountain became an important religious site in the year 720, when the Korean Buddhist Kiao Kak settled in the region and set up a shrine to Ksitigarbha, a bodhisattva who is known as a guardian of the earth and a protector of young children. Soon monks and nuns flocked to the area, and during the Tang dynasty there were said to be as many as 3000 devotees living in around 150 monasteries. There are still some 70 temples and monasteries, making Juihuashan a place of pilgrimage for many Chinese Buddhists.

From Anqing the river widens to form a slow-flowing stream that was once the home of the Yangtze's most endangered creature, the baiji or Chinese river dolphin. With its long beak, small eyes, low dorsal fin and broad, rounded pectoral fins, the baiji is easy to recognize. But few have the chance to see it these days, since its numbers are probably down to a handful. It once lived in two of the great lakes of the river basin, Dongting and Poyang, but these are too shallow now for this large creature, which is therefore found only on the lower Yangtze itself.

The Chinese are making huge conservation efforts to try to save the baiji dolphin. They have opened an oceanarium, a reserve and a number of conservation stations. They are also co-operating with international conservation bodies to plan improved measures. But the creature still seems to be in decline. It is a powerful symbol of how the authorities clearly need to move quickly to increase their stewardship of the river's fragile and fascinating habitat.

Around 100 km (60 miles) of winding river brings the traveller from Anqing to Wuhu, a transport hub, where railway lines and roads meet and there is a busy river port. As its name suggests, Wuhu was in ancient times a city of the Wu kingdom. Much later, under the Ming, it became a major trading centre, where large boats could dock and load up with cargoes of rice and other local produce. This tradition of trading made Wuhu well placed in the nineteenth century when Chinese cities started to be opened up to foreign trade, and a Treaty Port was established in 1876. Rice, tea and timber were the main commodities being bought and sold here.

Above: The baiji dolphin was once common enough to be a familiar symbol of the entire Yangtze and was seen along the length of the river, especially among dykes and sandbars. Now it is the most endangered of all the large aquatic mammals.

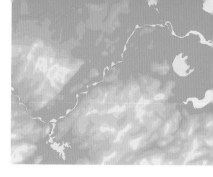

With the decline of foreign trade in the twentieth century, Wuhu was still well placed as a port and transport centre. The rice trade continued, and Wuhu developed heavy engineering industries and textile factories. It is still mainly an industrial city and little remains of its early history. One of its most famous buildings is the Mid-River Pagoda, which stands where the Qingyi River joins the Yangtze. It was built as a lighthouse and earned its name because it is said to stand precisely at the mid-point of the Yangtze's lower reaches.

Away from the main river highway of the Yangtze, with its big cargo ships and barges, the much narrower Qingyi River has an atmosphere more akin to a Chinese trading river of old. A jumble of bamboo rafts and small boats fills the water, and the place rings with the shouts of boatmen. Anything and everything is carried on these craft, from fresh vegetables to the bamboo steamers used to cook them. But many of the items seen hereabouts are to do with fishing – nets, baskets and other tackle – reminding one that even in this industrial city we are not far from the traditional lifestyle of the Yangtze fisherman.

Below: Small boats, like these sampans, are used for all sorts of functions, from fishing to local transport. The tiny craft look out of scale on the river's wide lower waters.

FISH AND FISHING

In this watery landscape, where it is impossible to travel any distance without coming across a river, canal, dyke or lake, fishing is a source of income and survival for many. More than 60 per cent of the total catch on the Yangtze comes from the river's lower reaches, where about half the fish caught are anchovies. Various species of carp, whitefish and catfish are also caught on the lower river.

But in recent years this activity has hit a problem. A combination of water pollution and over-fishing has led to a decline in fish stocks and seasonal bans on fishing. This is a massive blow to many who live by the river and depend on fishing for both income and food. But the government claims that the policy is working. Since the bans were imposed, the fish population is starting to rise once more. Nevertheless, there are still endangered species, such as the Chinese sturgeon (see page 101), and the whole river ecosystem needs to be continuously monitored, especially since the changes brought about by the Three Gorges Dam.

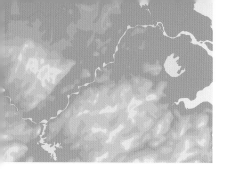

Meanwhile, during periods when the activity is permitted, a huge range of different fishing methods can be seen along the Long River. One of the most picturesque is now seldom seen on the Yangtze – fishing with trained cormorants. The tethered birds perch on the fisherman's bamboo raft at night-time before diving into the water and swimming under the surface until they make a catch. A rope around each bird's neck prevents it from swallowing its prey, which the bird brings back to the raft, when it is taken by the fisherman.

More common on the Yangtze are various forms of fishing with nets – bag-like fyke nets, drop nets, or long damming nets. The size of the mesh used in the nets varies. Too dense a mesh can cause problems, trapping juvenile fish before they have had a chance to breed. In some surveys, more than 60 per cent of the total catch has been made up of juvenile fish. Although the usual figure is much lower than this, it indicates that better regulation of the fishing industry is needed to make the stocks more sustainable. Other measures, such as improved overall management of the whole water ecosystem – lakes, dykes and canals, as well as the river itself – will also help prevent other kinds of fish joining the Chinese sturgeon and Chinese sucker as rare or endangered species.

NANJING – THE SOUTHERN CAPITAL

Some 96 km (60 miles) downstream of Wuhu is Nanjing, historically one of China's most important cities and still a metropolis of over 5 million people. By the Eastern Han period it had city walls, and Buddhist shrines came soon after. In subsequent centuries it was often the capital as different dynasties moved their base from one city to another. Palaces, fortresses and pagodas were built, and the place became notable as a centre of culture and the home of many famous writers during the Tang dynasty. The city was also capital under the Ming until 1420 and still boasts a number of towers and temples from this time, as well as the Ming city walls, which are the longest in the world, with some of the original city gates. The people of the Qing dynasty also enhanced the city, putting up structures such as the Jiming Si (Rooster Crow Temple). Nanjing's tree-lined streets, lakes and parkland still make it a pleasant place to relax. But some events in the city's life have been among the most traumatic in the whole of China's long history.

Below: In Nanjing, ancient shrines survive, with images of the Buddha in rows of niches. The statues date from the fifth century.

The first of these events was in 1850, when the Yangtze suffered the greatest crisis in its history, a crisis that was increasingly focused on Nanjing. The region suffered millions of deaths, a transformation of its culture, and devastation to many of its cities during the Taiping Rebellion, one of China's darkest hours. It began with discontent with China's Qing rulers. The Qing, who had ruled since 1644, had achieved some successes: they had opened up the country to foreign trade and increased prosperity. But this wealth was available to only a few. Western imported goods forced some native industries, such as textile weaving, into sharp decline. Many lost their jobs or incomes, and those who had an income were taxed punitively. Opium, the main foreign import, enslaved many to addiction, and a series of famines – partly caused by imperial neglect of irrigation and drainage systems – brought suffering and death.

Many of these problems were laid at the door of the Qing emperors. To make things worse, the Qing were not Chinese, but Manchus, from Manchuria in the northeast. More and more people

Above: Substantial sections of Nanjing's Ming dynasty city wall can still be found, running above the Qin Huai River, which flows into the Yangtze.

were convinced that these foreign rulers had little care for the interests of China. The country became a melting-pot, a cause waiting for a rebel.

Into this gathering storm came a visionary, Hong Xiuquan. Hong identified himself as the brother of Jesus Christ and was convinced that God had told him to rid China of demons. These demons must, he was sure, be the Qing. So he gathered a group of followers around him and planned a new regime, called Taiping Tianguo (Heavenly Kingdom of Great Peace).

Above: At night Nanjing is alive with neon, as the illuminated signs, fixed to buildings in a catalogue of architectural styles, flicker into dazzling life.

The kingdom was to be a theocracy, led by Hong himself with the help of four sub-kings, named after the four cardinal directions.

In many ways, what Hong proposed was fair – and, indeed, visionary. Private property would be abolished. The sexes would be granted equal status. Slavery would be banned. Opium would be outlawed. Cruel customs, from the binding of women's feet to infanticide, would come to an end. It was an attractive agenda, and many peasants, poor or dispossessed, rose to join Hong and his followers. They swept through Guangxi province with more and more people joining them as they went. Soon more were on their way down the Grand Canal towards the south, commandeering boats and picking up more support as they travelled towards the Yangtze. They seemed unstoppable.

By 1853 they were in Nanjing and established a capital there. The action was a sign that this was now a national movement with the ambition to transform the whole of China totally. They instituted many of their planned reforms, garnered more support, and went for an attack on Beijing. But try as they might, they could not oust the Qing from the capital, and the Taiping remained a southern kingdom, based by the Long River in Nanjing.

Taiping rule lasted for just over a decade, but was riven with divisions from the start. Hong was forever watching his back, convinced that the sub-kings would try to remove him. Increasingly convinced that the east king was a traitor, he had him killed and some 20,000 of his followers massacred in one night in 1856. Further atrocities followed while the Manchus continued to fight the rebels and millions were killed as one indecisive battle followed another.

In 1862, the rebels attacked Shanghai. This move turned the tide because of the Western traders and diplomats based here. Seeing at first hand the destruction caused by the rebellion and the threat to their livelihoods, the Westerners backed the Qing. They imported weapons from Europe for the imperial forces and provided commanders who trained them. The writing was on the wall for Hong and his followers.

Then the strengthened imperial army went on the attack. The year 1864 saw them surrounding Nanjing and laying siege to the city. Soon the rebels were on their knees, with supplies running low and a superior force ranged around the

Below: Small pagodas like this, now swamped by modern buildings, once dominated the skyline of the old city of Nanjing.

city walls. The imperial army blew up the city walls and took Nanjing. The place was devastated. Hong himself died of an illness as the chaos closed in around him.

It took years for Nanjing to recover, but in 1876 it became a Treaty Port and recovered its importance as a commercial centre. After the 1911 revolution, the city became the capital of the new republic of China and continued to thrive. A successful trading and financial quarter developed near the waterfront, and Nanjing traders became known the world over. A few of its buildings put up during this period still survive, but many of these offices, shops and wharves were destroyed when the typhoon of conflict hit Nanjing once more during the Sino-Japanese War of 1937–45. Nanjing saw the worst of this conflict before the Sino-Japanese War became part of World War II in 1941. Japan occupied much of eastern China and, as the capital, Nanjing bore the brunt of a vicious attack. As the Chinese government fled to Chongqing, the Japanese, with their slogan of 'Loot all! Burn all! Kill all!' descended on the city to carry out what became known as the rape of Nanjing. Much of the city was flattened, civilians were tied up and used for 'bayonet practice', and estimates of the casualties range from 300,000 to 400,000. Unsurprisingly, much of old Nanjing has been destroyed during the terrible times the city has experienced. But it is a resilient place, and there are still streets and districts where it is possible to find evidence of its periods of importance and prosperity. Some two-thirds of the Ming city wall

Above: Western and imperial troops gather outside the city walls of Nanjing during the Taiping Rebellion.

remains, up to 12 m (39 feet) high and punctuated with strong towers and gateways. These gates were major fortifications, as can still be seen at the grand Zhonghua Gate on the southern stretch of the wall. This was large enough to hold a 3000-man garrison, and an attacker had first of all to break through four sets of doors before gaining entrance – a virtually impossible task.

Ancient temples, both Buddhist and Confucian, and elegant pavilions provide some of the city's more peaceful sights. Many of these are to be found in the parkland to the east of the city centre, outside the old walls. Here there are lakes, and beyond them the land rises to a wooden hill called Zijin Shan (Purple Mountain) overlooking the bustle of the city. Standing here, one can appreciate how Nanjing embraces both the calm and the bustle, a place of contemplation but also of meetings and partings. A famous poem, 'Parting at a Wineshop in Nanjing', by the Tang dynasty writer Li Bai recalls such occasions by the river. In Vikram Seth's translation, the poem ends:

Above: Explosions rocked the streets of the city during the rape of Nanjing in 1937. Soon many of these streets were devastated by flames and smoke.

> *We Nanjing friends are here to see each other off.*
> *Those who must go, and those who don't, each drains his cup.*
> *Go ask the Yangtze, which of these two sooner ends:*
> *Its waters flowing east – the love of parting friends.*

ZHENJIANG

About an hour downriver from Nanjing, Zhenjiang is surrounded on three sides by wooded mountains and still keeps some of its old cobbled streets and alleys, together with pagodas built in the Tang and Yuan dynasties. One of the city's most famous buildings is Jin Shan (Golden Hill Temple), with its pagoda dating originally from the Sui dynasty but rebuilt many times since. Inside the temple are relics, including a bronze drum, said to have belonged to the great military leader Zhuge Liang. Richly gilded statues, including the 18 *luohan*, or followers of the Buddha are the most stunning objects in the temple's Buddha hall.

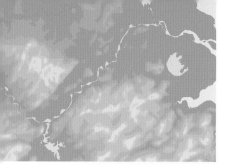

As these remains suggest, Zhenjiang is an ancient city, the site of a fortress where guards kept the river free of pirates. The town was a notable river-crossing place in the time of the first emperor, the capital of the Wu in the Three Kingdoms period, and well known for its textile production in Song and Yuan times. During the reign of the Yuan emperor Kubilai Khan (Shizu), Marco Polo visited Zhenjiang, praising its industry and commerce, and noting that the people produced a quantity of silk and brocade. It is still a productive industrial city today.

But Zhenjiang is best known as the place where the Grand Canal joins the Yangtze, making it one of the most important transport hubs on the river. Like other great engineering projects, such as the Great Wall, the canal was not created at one time. Sections were dug in different periods and for different purposes. It began in the Three Kingdoms, when the rulers of Wu wanted an invasion route towards the kingdom of Ji, to the north. Later, the Sui dynasty extended the canal to connect the capital, Luoyang (later Beijing), with the rice and grain fields of the south. An army of workers – conscripted for the task – carried out this gargantuan task between 605 and 609. In so doing, they linked the Yellow and Yangtze rivers and created the longest canal in the world. Under the Yuan, the canal was further improved and given a more direct route to make grain supply to the north more efficient.

The canal is still used today, dredged and made navigable again after a period of decline in the nineteenth century. It is still used for trade and, increasingly, for tourism, though old low stone bridges and narrow reaches make parts of it passable only to small, flat-bottomed boats. It also performs a role in water management, sending water from the Yangtze northwards to improve the land around the capital.

TAI HU – RICE AND TOURISM

In the lowlands south of the river, to the south of Wuxi and west of Suzhou, lies Tai Hu, another of the great lakes of the Yangtze region. Close to other big cities, including Hangzhou and Shanghai, the lake is a favourite spot for tourists and there are parks around many of its shores. A favourite trip is to take the ferry to Sanshan (Three Hills), one of around ninety islands in the lake. Here one can admire tall statues of the Buddha, watch the monkeys and enjoy views of the rest of the lake from one of the temples or pavilions.

Tai Hu is vast – nearly 2340 square km (900 square miles) in area – but shallow – its average depth is only around 1.8–2.13m (6–7 feet). The huge and tranquil lake is near the centre of the

delta, so is surrounded by fertile, silty land. The region's farmers have seen an opportunity in this fertility and have reclaimed parts of the lakeshore for rice fields and fish ponds, for the lake abounds in silvery fish that are valued and tasty food.

The delta's farmers are keen to find opportunities like this because they have, since the late 1980s, been released from the tightest shackles imposed by the communist system. The new

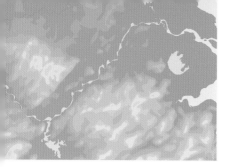

system rewards high output with better pay, and they are free to organize their farms in the way that provides the highest productivity. The delta was already a region of intensive farming. The watery rice fields are densely packed, flooded rectangles that make a strong pattern between their protective dykes – and even these are planted with mulberries or sugar cane to increase productivity still further. The fields themselves can sometimes support three harvests a year – two of rice and one of wheat. As a result of this activity, some of the delta farmers have become the highest paid in China. But they do not call themselves capitalists, for the state still owns the land that they cultivate.

YANGZHOU – CITY OF THE SALT BARONS

Not far from Zhenjiang is one of the canal's other notable cities, Yangzhou, which is slightly to the north of the river. It is a place famous for beautiful gardens and for women who are either beautiful or wise, or perhaps both, according to which folklorist you believe. Its sights have, fittingly for a city close to the lower Yangtze, a cosmopolitan air, for there is an early mosque and the tomb of its founder Puhaddin, a descendant of the prophet Muhammad, who lived in Yangzhou for ten years in the thirteenth century.

The importance of Yangzhou in ancient times was its role in the salt trade. The city was a major collecting-point for cargoes of salt, which came here from salt pans along the coast. Huge salt cargoes travelled upstream on junks from Yangzhou, taking advantage of the Yangtze's various tributaries to distribute the commodity to people over a vast area. This business made fortunes for the city's merchants, who built large houses and headquarters here. These men were famous for their wealth during the Ming and Qing dynasties. Some became renowned art collectors, others were the patrons of scholars or writers, still others blew their fortunes on high living and luxurious houses. Whether tasteful or extravagant, they were well known all over southern China.

Yangzhou is truly a place of canals – not just the Grand Canal itself, but a network of smaller channels running parallel to the city's grid of streets. Crossed by bridges (mostly of concrete today, although in former times they were built of stone), they give the place its special character. Their watery presence also reminds visitors that the place was once wetter still. The most ancient accounts of the Yangtze say that the sea once came up to Yangzhou, although today the city is some 130 km (80 miles) from the sea as the crow flies. Silt must have been building up here for millennia, slowly creating the land through which the river now flows on the final, wide, slow stretch of its journey towards the ocean.

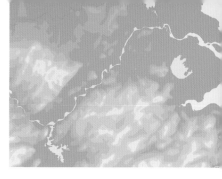

For much of this stretch the Yangtze is, above all, a working river, full of large cargo ships and lined with industrial towns and cities. One such is Nantong, a port city with vast factories producing textiles, machinery, and other goods. Overlooked by visitors and represented by a small dot on most maps, it is still a city of over 7 million people. Another such city is Baoshan, smaller in size but boasting China's largest steelworks, fed via the river with coal from northern China and iron ore from Australia.

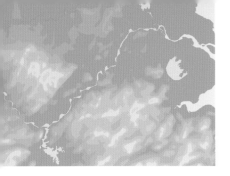

Cities like these seem to be totally wedded to the matter-of-fact world of industry. Yet they would not be here if it were not for the river, which has been a lifeline to them for centuries. So even these industrial cities have their river legends. Near Nantong there was said in the Song dynasty to be a Buddhist monk who could protect you from water demons. Boatmen brought him offerings and prayed to his spirit after his death. Soon they built a temple in his honour on top of a hill called Lang Shan (Wolf Hill). To this day models of different types of river boat are kept in the temple's hall.

Below: The wooded slopes of Lang Shan, east of Nantong, are home to several buildings with the Cao Gong Zhu Memorial Temple at the summit.

BOATS ON THE YANGTZE

Nowadays on the lower reaches one is most likely to see large, modern boats, from big cruisers and passenger-carriers to still larger cargo ships and barges. But occasionally the traditional craft of the river are still used. The best known of these are the junks, but there are also smaller vessels, such as sampans and wupans.

The Chinese built huge junks for ocean sailing. Those traditionally used on the rivers are smaller, but similar in many ways. Junks have pontoon-style hulls – in other words, the structure is divided into a number of watertight compartments so that if one section is holed, the ship does not sink. The hulls are flat-bottomed and have a characteristic squared-off profile at bow and stern. There can be up to three masts, and the sails are usually square and typically supported with thin wooden battens. These battens have several uses: they keep the sail flat (even if it is made of thin, poor-quality sail cloth), allow it to be gathered up or dropped at speed, and provide a sort of ladder for sailors to climb aloft. The traditional uses for junks were diverse – from warfare to carrying cargo. Today there is still a variety of junks on the river, though they are nearly all motor-powered – the sight of the beautiful bamboo-battened sails is becoming rarer and rarer.

There are still thousands of smaller vessels too, with their curved-roofed cabins and long stern poles or oars. These boats are named after the number of planks in their hull – the wupan (five planks) and sampan (or sanpan, three planks). The larger wupan could carry many passengers quite great distances along the river – for example, ferrying people through the Three Gorges, or taking them from Yichang down to Wuhan. Smaller sampans would go shorter distances, carrying a few people, a family, a load of local produce, or a fisherman's catch.

Junks and sampans could be adapted in all sorts of ways. A sampan could become a houseboat. The famous 'singsong girls' of Nanjing entertained their male clients on board such boats – mostly tiny vessels with just enough room for the young woman and her customer. On a larger scale, a junk could do service as a floating hotel. This ingenuity continues today, with boats serving as floating houses, shops and even cinemas, as every aspect of life is lived out on the waters of the Long River, and vessels congregate everywhere, not just in the docks of places like Baoshan.

Above: A procession of junks sails up the river at Nanjing. It is now rare to see so many of these old-style craft together.

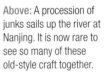

Looking downriver from these vast and busy docks, a lighthouse signals the confluence of the Huangpu River. Near where it joins the Yangtze is the country's greatest port, the greatest city in the Yangtze region, and one of the most famous in the world – Shanghai.

SHANGHAI

Few cities have such a notorious reputation as Shanghai. Home to opium addicts and speculators, gamblers and pimps, big spenders and get-rich-quick schemers, it seemed in the early twentieth century to exemplify the pitfalls and horrors that awaited the naive Westerner as he stepped off the boat into China for the first time. Go there, people said, and you will be fleeced; go there, and you will be shanghaied – drugged and carried off into the navy, slavery or worse. Western visitors needed that semi-mythical but useful authority, an 'old China hand', to show them round the place – and even locals had to be on their guard.

Shanghai was a melting-pot of cultures. It was not very big when the Europeans started to arrive in 1842 – it had a local importance and was defended by walls, that was all. And those

walls were undefended when British troops turned up, attacked the city in the climax of the first opium war, and forced the Chinese to begin trading with them. The French followed in 1847, and in a few years there was an international community trading from buildings along the Bund, the embankment that lines the waterfront of the Huangpu, the small river that snakes its way through the city and flows into the Yangtze estuary.

These foreigners had the unusual privilege of extraterritoriality. In other words, although they lived in China, they were not subject to Chinese law. Their district was legally a small piece of Britain, or France, transported to the other side of the world. British policemen and soldiers patrolled the British concession, French, Italian, American and Japanese troops were seen in their respective sections. European gunboats guarded European interests on the river itself. As well as legal immunity, the Europeans enjoyed their own clubs – the Shanghai Club on the Bund had a bar 43 m (141 feet) long – and their own shops supplying everything from London gin to the London *Times*. And many of the European rich here led lives of pleasure underpinned by the commerce on the river, lives that could be dominated by the racecourse and the club – or by the gambling den and the brothel.

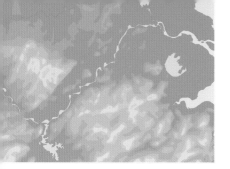

The British were keen to deal in opium, fuelling an addiction that had already taken hold, for although the Westerners imported the drug by the tonne, much also came from the Chinese interior. There was also a booming business in the other typical Yangtze products, such as tea, rhubarb, silk, tung oil and porcelain.

The Chinese began to blend opium with tobacco and smoke the mixture in the seventeenth century. The habit probably started in Southeast Asia and Taiwan before spreading to the mainland, and it was already a problem there by the early eighteenth century – the authorities made the first of many attempts to ban the drug in 1729. By the beginning of the nineteenth century opium was being smoked pure and was being imported to China in large quantities. The British were the major importers, bringing into the country such large quantities of opium from India that, by the 1830s, opium imports actually made up half of the goods that the British sold in China.

The trade was all-pervasive. There were millions of addicts and thousands of people, from dealers to financiers, involved in supplying them. According to one estimate, there may have been 15 million opium addicts in China by 1890. Major cities such as Shanghai and Chongqing had thousands of opium dens where people could smoke themselves into oblivion, together with shops and wandering peddlers who sold opium from wayside stalls.

The Qing rulers of China repeatedly tried to put a stop to this poisonous trade, and the opium war of 1839–42 was waged between them and the British, who had enough of a vested interest to fight for the trade. The British won the war, but already there were plenty of native suppliers too. Deeply implicated as they were, the British cannot shoulder the entire blame for enslaving the Chinese to opium.

Could this fragile and headlong mix of prosperity and vice last? Shanghai took a pounding in the Taiping Rebellion (see page 135), but it recovered rapidly and continued as a centre of commerce into the early twentieth century. What is more, it benefited from the rebellion because, in the aftermath of the destruction of Nanjing, merchants needed a replacement port on the Yangtze. Shanghai filled the gap, and it soon had more ships in its harbours than London. There were two main foreign zones in the city – the International Settlement, effectively controlled by the British, and the French Concession. Both of these burgeoned.

The city survived the revolution of 1911, when the last emperor, the young Puyi, was ousted from power and the Republic of China was established – first under Nationalist leader Sun

Above: Away from the grand stone buildings on the main streets, the European concessions of early twentieth-century Shanghai were full of narrow streets with wooden shops and houses.

Yatsen and then under the first Nationalist president, Yuan Shikai. But soon after World War I, the seeds of change were sown. The very cosmopolitan atmosphere of Shanghai fostered an appetite for radicalism and change. So too did the exploitation of Chinese workers by the rich. In a city where a few mainly foreign people had access to wealth, privilege and a conspicuous high life, while most Chinese lived in poverty, hunger and often slavery, it is not surprising that the latter eventually longed for change.

And so it was in Shanghai in 1921 that the Chinese Communist Party was founded and held its first congress. The communists had an uneasy relationship with the ruling nationalist Kuomintang – the two organizations tried to cooperate but there was also bitter fighting. But all this became irrelevant during the Sino-Japanese War, for Shanghai fell to the Japanese in 1937. It only really recovered when communist leader Deng Xiaoping introduced a series of economic reforms in the late twentieth century, and when still further economic changes once more opened up China to contact and trade with the West, allowing Shanghai to develop into the twenty-first-century city of today.

Parts of old Shanghai still remain. The Bund preserves its selection of 1930s' neoclassical company headquarters. The old Chinese city is still a maze of narrow streets crammed with

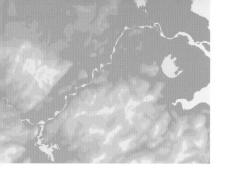

houses and featuring the Yu Gardens (designed in the Ming dynasty) and their bazaar, packed with shops, restaurants and teahouses and crowded with people. Faguo Zujie, formerly the French Concession, offers a feast of neoclassical and art deco buildings, as well as modern department stores.

But today, for good or bad, Shanghai is dominated by developments that have taken place since 1988. This was the year in which the city's revenue arrangements with the capital were revised. Instead of paying nearly all its revenue into the centralized economy of Beijing, Shanghai was allowed to give a fixed sum, leaving the remainder for investment in the city. A rash of bridges, tunnels, roads, factories and other new buildings was the visible result, as the city developed a new and vigorous economy.

Most notably, the city expanded into Pudong, a former area of farmland to the east of the Huangpu River. This has been taken over by a new airport and a collection of office towers and lower-rise buildings that are familiar from modern photographs of the Shanghai skyline.

Most famous and most extraordinary of these is the Oriental Pearl Television Tower, with its concrete pylons, spherical observation lounges and sky-pointing tip. It seems to point to the future as well as the sky, perhaps to a time in which global communications will be far more important to China than the physical movement of goods up and down the Yangtze. But in the meantime Pudong's developments include a new port, from which vessels can travel both up the river and out into the East China Sea.

THE PASSAGE TO THE SEA

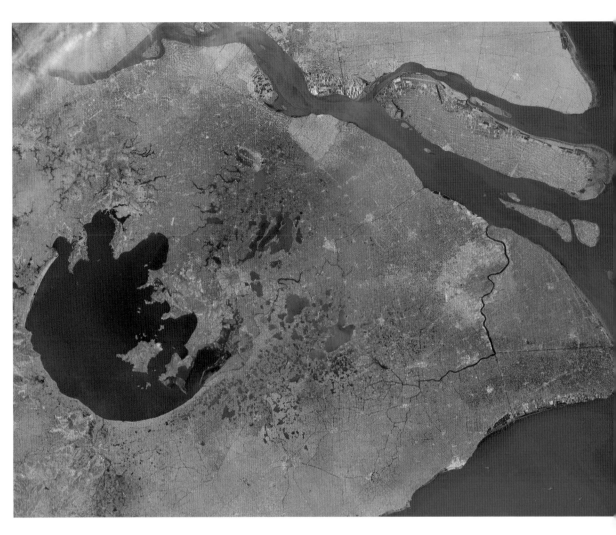

Large, deep-draft ships were not always able to make this passage, for the channel was shallow and beset with sandbanks and mudflats. This was not a problem for Chinese boatmen, whose junks could sail in a mere 3 m (10 feet) of water or even less. It became an issue only when foreign powers wanted to sail up the river in the nineteenth century, for European boats have a far deeper draft. Many European craft got stuck in the mud, especially at the Wusong Kou, the place where the Huangpu joins the Yangtze.

The Wusong Kou is a bar of mud and sand deposited by the Huangpu into the mouth of the Yangtze. By the time of the Treaty Ports it had built up into a seemingly immovable sticky barrier on the river bottom. It transformed a channel that was elsewhere some 15 m (50 feet) deep into one that in places provided only about 3.5 m (11 or 12 feet) of water for river craft. European ships regularly got stuck, and ship-owners became frustrated. But the Chinese accepted the nuisance – after all, their own flat-bottomed ships were ideally suited to making this difficult passage. European sea captains had to put up with the bar until 1910, when, on the eve of the revolution, the Chinese finally cut a channel through the mud, making it far easier for foreign deep-draft ships to enter the river.

Above: A satellite photograph shows the mouth of the Yangtze. At the top are the river's vast estuary and the rectangular Chongming Island. Shanghai shows as a paler mass just south of the river.

Opposite, top: Sun Yatsen, often known as the father of the Chinese nation, was the nationalist leader and founder of the Kuomintang (Nationalist Party).

Opposite, bottom: Floodlighting on the waterfront shows that many of the old buildings of Shanghai's Bund survive.

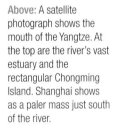

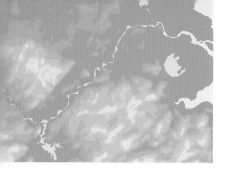

At the Wusong Kou we are at the very mouth of the Yangtze, and the long downstream journey taken by this book is almost at an end. Seen from the southwestern bank, the river mouth seems to stretch for miles across, a vast sheet of water, full of ships, that can stretch into the distance like a silver, sun-lit sheet of metal, or disappear in a cloud of suffocating fog.

But impressive as it is, this is not the whole width of the Yangtze because the estuary contains a huge island, Chongming. Some 32 km (20 miles) long by about 6.5 km (4 miles) wide, this island has been built up by silt deposited by the river. Home to many people who have been moved from the Three Gorges, this is a place of fertile soil where rice and cotton are farmed. In the long history of the river, Chongming is a 'new' place, an island that has gradually been built up since historical records began – and it is still steadily growing.

Moving down the estuary, the buildings thin out. There is still industry – a few chimneys, some cooling towers, cranes. And the water is still busy with boats – small fishing vessels vying for space with vast cargo-carriers, the old and new China side by side. And then the river's mouth widens still further, leaving Chongming behind, until Zhong Sha (Middle Sand Light) with its flashing lamp, marks the official point where river and ocean meet, the river's vast body of water merges with the sea, and the voyager leaves behind at last the seemingly eternal presence of the Long River.

And here it seems as eternal as it did among the frozen glaciers and pebbly channels of the headwaters in Tibet and Qinghai. The lower Yangtze is a workplace, but it still has a vastness and power that can take the breath away. Tu Fu, probably China's greatest poet, felt this, and he knew the Long River and lived by it and travelled it. In exile upriver, he remembered his brother, from whom he had not heard for years and who lived near the mouth and near the ocean, within range, the poet imagined, of sea-serpents. Tu Fu longed, as so many have longed, to travel the length of the river, and to find his long-lost brother among the clouds and the sea mirages:

> My shadow sticks to trees where gibbons scream,
> But my spirit whirls by the showers sea-serpents breathe.
> Let me go down next year with the spring waters
> And search for you to the end of the white clouds in the East.

Above: An old engraving shows Tu Fu, author of a number of poems set by the banks of China's greatest river.

Opposite: At the mouth of the Yangtze ships from the East China Sea begin their journey inland to one of the river's major ports.

ACKNOWLEDGEMENTS

Amongst the numerous accounts of the Yangtze River, the author has found the following especially useful and inspiring:

Bonavia, Judy, *The Yangzi River and the Three Gorges* (Odyssey, 1999)

Lynn, Madeleine, Y*angzi River: The Wildest, Wickedest River on Earth* (OxfordUniversity Press Hong Kong, 1997)

Slyke, Lyman P., Van *Yangtse: Nature, History and the River* (Addison-Wesley,1988)

Winchcester, Simon, *The River at the Centre of the World* (Viking, 1997)

Wong, How Man, *Exploring the Yangtse, China's Longest River* (Odyssey, 1989)

Quotations from ancient Chinese poetry have been taken with thanks from:

Graham, A. C., *Poems of the Late T'ang* (Penguin, 1965)

Seth, Vikram, *Three Chinese Poets* (Faber and Faber, 1992)

PICTURE CREDITS

BBC Worldwide would like to thank the following individuals and organizations for providing photographs and for permission to reproduce copyright material.

Special thanks are due to Liu Liqun of Chinastock for his valuable contribution to the picture research, for providing archive material and specially-commissioned photography.

While every effort has been made to trace and acknowledge copyright holders, we would like to apologize should there be any errors or omissions.

Ancient Art and Architecture 134; Heather Angel 5 (fourth row right), 30, 126, 130, 131; George Chan 1, 3, 4, 5 (second row left inset), 5 (fourth row left), 5 third row right, 9, 12, 16; ChinaStock 23 (Liu Qijun), 24,(Ru Suichu) 36, (Liu Liqun) 45 (Liu Liqun), 55 (Mu Fang Kui), 65 (Liu Liqun), 70, 74 (Liu Liqun), 76, 80, 100 (Liu Liqun), 104 (Liu Liqun), 111 (Liu Liqun), 117 (Lu Houmin), 119, 120 (Liu Liqun), 124 (Liu Liqun),129 (Liu Xiaoyang), 135, 144 (Liu Xiaoyang), 150 above, 152; Corbis 4 below, 5 top row left, 5 second row left, 5 fourth row left inset, 5 top row right, 5 second row right, 18, 19, 27, 28, 32, 33 above, 33 below, 38, 41, 52, 53, 56, 57, 58, 63, 68, 71, 72, 73 above, 73 below, 75, 81, 82, 83, 85, 88, 91, 96, 98,101,102, 103, 106, 107, 108, 110, 127, 133, 137, 138, 141, 143, 146, 147, 154; Document China 51, 87; Eye Ubiquitous 37, 42; Getty 8, 46, 67, 78; Sally and Richard Greenhill 150 below; Amar Grover 34; Lonely Planet 136; Magnum 5 third row, right, 93, 118, 145; John S. Murray 60; Ancil Nance 21, 26, 29; National Geographic 43, 44, 49, 61; Panos Pictures 2; Science Photo Library 151; Sovfoto 17, 22, 64, 77, 95, 109, 122, 123, 142, 153; Still Pictures 132; Ian Teh 5 third row left, 92, 99, 114; Tibet Images 31; Topham 47, 139,149; United States Geological Survey 15.

INDEX